Role MONTAGE

A Creative New Way to Discover the **LEADER** Within You

Jan M. Schmuckler, PhD

Role Montage:

A Creative New Way to Discover the LEADER Within You

Copyright © 2016 Jan M. Schmuckler, PhD

All rights reserved. This book may not be reproduced in any form, in whole or in part (beyond the copying permitted by US Copyright Law, Section 107, "fair use" in teaching or research, Section 108, certain library copying, or in published media by reviewers in limited excerpts), without written permission from the author.

Published by Lakeshore Press.

Softcover ISBN: 978-0-9973937-0-5
Ebook ISBN: 978-0-9973937-1-2

Disclaimer

The author and the publisher specifically disclaim any liability, loss or risk, personal or otherwise, which is incurred as a consequence, directly or indirectly, of use and application of any of the contents of this book.

The names used throughout this book are fictional, although the circumstances are taken from actual clients, research participants, and leaders.

Dedication

In loving memory of those who taught me self-awareness, leadership, and generosity of spirit:

Irene M. Schmuckler, my mother

Edie W. Seashore, my mentor

Vivienne L. Crawford, my neighbor

Contents

PREFACE 1
   Origins of Role Montage 2
   Emerging Leaders 4

INTRODUCTION 5

CHAPTER 1 WHAT IS A ROLE MONTAGE? 9
   In This Chapter 9
   Why Leadership Is So Difficult Today 12
   Importance of Values for Leadership 13
   Roots of Role Montage 14
   Role Montage, a Tool for Self-Awareness 15
   Role Montage, a Diagnostic Tool 17
   Conclusion 17
   Chapter 1 Exercises 19
   Exercise A 19
   Exercise B 20
   Finding Your Inspiration 21

CHAPTER 2 SELF-AWARENESS AND THE SUCCESSFUL LEADER 23
   In This Chapter 23
   Definition of Self-Awareness 26
   What Makes a Successful Leader? 27
   Developing Self-Awareness 28
   A Personal Mentor Example 33
   Links to Emotional Intelligence 35
   How Self-Awareness Impacts Leadership 37
   Conclusion 39
   Chapter 2 Exercises 40
   Exercise A 40
   Exercise B 41

  Exercise C 41
  Building Self-Awareness 43

CHAPTER 3 THE ROLE MONTAGE ADVANTAGE 45
  In This Chapter 45
  Role Montage Example 46
  Personal Example 49
  Negative People in Role Montage 50
  Why Role Montage Is a Powerful Tool 51
  Few Role Models for Women 53
  Conclusion 54
  Chapter 3 Exercises 55
  Exercise A 55
  Exercise B 56
  Exercise C 56
  Are You Ready for Role Montage? 57

CHAPTER 4 HOW TO DESIGN A ROLE MONTAGE 59
  In This Chapter 59
  Starting a Role Montage 60
  Instructions for Completing a Role Montage 61
  Questions to Consider 62
  Mapping Guide 63
  What to Do Next 65
  Conclusion 66
  Chapter 4 Exercises 68
  Designing Your Role Montage 68

CHAPTER 5 PERSONAL APPLICATION OF ROLE MONTAGE 77
  In This Chapter 77
  Two Principal Practices 78
  Meditation Practice 80
  Zazen Meditation 81
  Finding a Quiet Space 82

Reflection Practice 83
Self-Observation and Learning from Mistakes 85
Reading, Observation, and Imitation 87
Physical Practices 88
Conclusion 88
Chapter 5 Exercises 90
Exercise A 90
Enhancing Personal Application Practices with Role Montage 92

CHAPTER 6 APPLYING WHAT YOU LEARNED IN THE WORKPLACE 93
In This Chapter 93
Team Building 94
Workshops and Training 96
Coaching and Consulting 97
Feedback 100
Conclusion 104
Chapter 6 Exercises 105
Toolkit for Learning about Self 105

APPENDICES 109
About the Appendices 111

Appendix A—Values Exercise 112
    Exercise 1 112
    Values List 113
    Exercise 2 114
    Values and Feedback Exercise 114

Appendix B—Role Montage Worksheet Example 116
    Exercise A 116
    Exercise B 116

Appendix C—Role Montage for the Ages 119

Appendix D—Forms for Getting Feedback 123
    Form 1—How to Choose Your Feedback Raters 124
    Form 2—Request for Feedback Form 126
    Form 3—Possible Questionnaire 127

Appendix E—Prototypes of Role Montage Pictures 128

Appendix F—For Coaches and Consultants:
    How to Use Role Montage Practice 134

Acknowledgments 137

About the Author 141

Notes 142

Preface

Have you ever wished you could create the perfect business partner, employer, spouse, or friend by combining the best attributes of people you know (or would like to know), successful individuals you've met, or historical figures you've read about? If you've done this little mental exercise, then you've experienced a form of "role montage." So what is a role montage?

Simply put, role montage is an internalized image of the leader you aspire to be. It's a mental picture you create by piecing together both imagined and physical images of the best, most appropriate characteristics of those individuals you admire, respect, or want to emulate. As one president from my dissertation said, "I think what you do is you put together bits and pieces of what looks to you as good and then gradually try to find and develop your own style." All leaders can use this idea.

Once you've created this internal, mental image (that is, in your "mind's eye") of the leader you aspire to be, you then use this self-visualized image as a roadmap to guide you toward becoming that more effective, self-aware leader. It's that simple. And if you fully engage with the technique, it can even be a life-changing exercise.

ORIGINS OF ROLE MONTAGE

In the early 1970s I moved to the San Francisco Bay area to become the program director for twelve youth programs in three different states. Since I was new to the area I didn't have any women mentors or role models to support me as I faced the challenges of my new, stressful job. For women working in male-dominated fields at that time, it was par for the course not to have a female role model or mentor in most high-level jobs. I wanted someone to guide me when I needed to make a difficult decision or help me navigate my way through the often challenging federal grant system.

I had better luck finding mentors and role models later in my career among the women professors and deans as I worked toward my doctoral degree. Still, I was surprised to find during my dissertation research that even successful women, including female college presidents, didn't have traditional role models or mentors to rely on. Instead, many of these women found creative ways to get the mentoring and coaching support they needed by relying on internalized images they'd created for themselves of significant figures from their personal lives, from their formal education experiences, or even wholly created using their imagination.

My informal dissertation advisor at the time, Dr. Lillian Cartwright,[1] was intrigued by the various roles women experienced in their lives and had conducted her own research on the topic using the experiences of women physicians. As noted, my own research used women college presidents and when Dr. Cartwright and I compared notes, we found similar results within both groups. Therefore, we developed the idea of role montage.

I expanded the concept through my interviews of college presidents, asking a cross-section of the participants if they had used what I characterized as a role montage process to support their leadership path. Once the study participants understood the concept, they agreed that a less formalized version of the role montage self-visualization process had helped them and they agreed that the concept could be a powerful tool to help women develop their leadership potential.

Although many years have elapsed since this initial research project, the idea of role montage has remained an essential part of my consulting practice. It is a concept that I have continually expanded and improved on over the years. The role montage process is a valuable tool, regardless of gender.

This book demonstrates that a great number of the leaders who participated in the supporting research for this book agree that using role montage is a helpful development tool. Several other focus groups I conducted later in my research and professional practice also support the usefulness of the role montage process.

EMERGING LEADERS

My purpose in writing this book is to introduce the concept of role montage to a wider audience, especially among the many young, emerging leaders who are looking for ways to achieve their future leadership goals. Role montage exploration is also a valuable tool for well-established leaders searching for a creative, individually driven technique that will further build their careers or achieve some specific goals.

I believe everyone has a role montage within them; whether they know it or not. Leaders choosing the role montage process have the advantage of a continuing, real-time source of support for their choices and decisions as leaders. My ultimate goal is for my readers to experience this book as if they were sitting in my living room in a cozy chair surrounded by all the leaders I've interviewed. I hope they will find the book inspiring and will use it to guide their own leadership and self-awareness exploration throughout their careers!

Introduction

 Role Montage: A Creative New Way to Discover the LEADER Within You asks its readers to open their minds and hearts to a new idea for leadership development and self-awareness exploration. The new concept of role montage describes a lifelong process of collecting values, ideas, and characteristics from people, whether real or imagined, from any source (books, movies, television shows, blog posts, magazine articles), and then internalizing an idealized image based on this self-created montage. This book offers readers an innovative way of thinking about how to use this role montage to build leadership and self-awareness capabilities.

The book is written for anyone with an interest in learning about themselves and their potential as a leader and is especially directed toward emerging leaders, both men and women. Although my interviews were conducted exclusively with women, the ideas and techniques in this book apply to all people. Role montage practice will help all leaders delve deeply into what makes or hinders them from being successful leaders. Whether a leader has formally identified a role model or mentor, the work of creating a role montage study is a valuable way to understand and, most important, take action to follow a leadership path.

This book offers the reader all you need to get started building your own role montage; it includes an extended definition of role montage and how the process is used to build self-awareness and leadership potential. Detailed instructions are included on how to develop a montage picture and then apply your discoveries to both your personal and professional life.

At the end of each chapter, you'll find exercises to personalize and then apply what you've learned in the chapters. You'll find illustrations and samples that explain the concepts drawn from both my own consulting and coaching practice and directly out of the formal studies I've conducted. The names assigned to the role montages are, of course, entirely fictitious. If anyone recognizes themselves in the stories, I hope they feel honored.

The role montage you ultimately create will allow you to build your own distinctive leadership capability and will become the solid foundation on which you build future success. I hope your journey is an exciting one full of humor, success, and variety.

My journey has been stimulating, provocative, and full of wisdom. I especially like reflecting on the changes in my role montage and how the changes correspond to my own growth and development as a leader. I hope you will find the same short- and long-term value in these pages and that you'll use these role montage exercises to enhance your leadership abilities on the road to becoming the leader you always wanted to be.

Chapter 1
WHAT IS A ROLE MONTAGE?

In This Chapter

- Why Leadership Is So Difficult Today

- Importance of Values for Leadership

- Roots of Role Montage

- Role Montage, a Tool for Self-Awareness

- Role Montage, a Diagnostic Tool

- Conclusion

- Chapter 1 Exercises

The concept of a role montage first emerged from a series of interviews I did in 1979 with women leaders as part of my PhD dissertation research. Throughout my career, it's a concept that has kept my interest and is a tool I have used personally to guide my own leadership journey. As the sidebar quote from cultural anthropologist Mary Catherine Bateson suggests, a role montage allows you to create a new and meaningful picture by weaving together multiple models from many different threads of your life.

Essentially, a role montage is an instrument that allows both emerging and established leaders to create an internalized image of the leader they wish to be. It's a process that involves piecing together the best, most appropriate characteristics of someone you admire, respect, or want to emulate and then applying these characteristics to your leadership journey.

> *I believe in the need for multiple models, so that it is possible to weave something new from many different threads.*
>
> —Mary Catherine Bateson

Think of it as creating a "mind's eye" vision (or version) of yourself. This self-created composite picture can be built from internalized words, actions, images, attributes, or values of anyone you have encountered during the course of your life. In the story of Ashley that follows, note how she thought about the people who influenced her and the role models she used to develop her leadership capabilities.

CHAPTER 1

In 2011, I graduated from Stanford University with an MBA and was immediately hired as a mid-level leader at Games-R-Us, a start-up gaming company. I felt stuck in my job, because I wasn't promoted for over two years, and my team of young managers wasn't as committed as I wanted. I realized I needed some inspiration and guidance to move my career forward.

One day as I was driving home from work, I heard a podcast about revolutionary politician Nelson Mandela. He had always inspired me with his leadership and his courage. I suspected that I'd be a better leader if I emulated Mandela's consensus-seeking, forward-looking approach.

I remembered the first time I heard of his resistance and resilience in prison. His story reminded me of my grandmother. When I was a little girl, Nana told me stories about her childhood in the war camps. Over and over, she admonished me, "Never give up." Sitting me on her lap, Nana looked into my eyes and repeated, "You are strong, and you can accomplish whatever you want to do."

I also thought about my high school civics teacher. Mrs. Schmidt encouraged me to run for student body president. After I won the elections, Mrs. S became my counselor and confidante. I remembered sitting in her office, talking about how to be a just and fair-minded leader.

As I thought about the words and deeds of the great South African leader, Nana's intense courage, and Mrs. S's steady demeanor, I also remembered my dad and how he would say, "That's my girl" after every swim meet, whether I won or lost. Health and exercise are important values for me.

By the time I got home and fixed something to eat, I said to myself, "I can do it. It'll be tough, but I'm up for it. I'll work with my team, be successful, and get a promotion.

Without realizing it, Ashley produced a role montage that she used as a guide for her leadership journey.

WHY LEADERSHIP IS SO DIFFICULT TODAY

The current pace of change is more rapid, urgent, and turbulent than ever before, and the business issues encountered by leaders are increasingly complex and multifaceted. Such complexity forces today's leaders to be keenly aware of the important knowledge and insight needed to be an effective leader.[2] Even knowledge gained in a traditional MBA or executive leadership program sometimes no longer seems relevant to today's leaders. With the pace so fast, leaders spend little time on self-development and personal growth. Organizations are also reluctant to provide time and money for developing their leaders.

Global workforce demographics are quickly changing the nature of leadership. The coming of age of the Millennial generation, who are typically comfortable with blurring the lines between leadership at home and leadership in the workplace, demonstrates this changing leadership landscape. These new leaders want a lot of playtime both at home and at work. This attitude puts them at odds with older "nose to the grindstone" generations and even Boomers who are sympathetic to these work-life balance ideas but don't always act on these preferences. Clearly, there are many positive values that each generation can share in this continuing conversation.

IMPORTANCE OF VALUES FOR LEADERSHIP

Today's leaders must be nimble and multidimensional while staying true to their core values. This requires being in touch with their deepest values through a keen sense of self-awareness. It's not that difficult to begin the process of developing self-awareness. Just think about the values you hold dear and consider where they come from in your life. If you need an easy tool to help you do this, I've provided a fairly simple values exercise in Appendix A that will guide you. Use this exercise to provide clarity about what you care about and consider important in your life.

Role montage taps into this essential need for self-awareness. It supplies internal images and patterns of behaviors that allows a new generation of leaders to lead with competence, compassion, and trust. Leaders who have developed this level of self-awareness have greater followership from those they manage due to their demonstrated clarity of values.

ROOTS OF ROLE MONTAGE

While the concepts outlined in this book have their roots in my PhD research, much of the content of this book is drawn from a set of interviews I did in 2009 and 2010 with forty-three leaders. These leaders were told they could cite anyone, including leaders they knew personally or had read about and contemporary or historical figures whose leadership story had inspired or influenced them.

Some of the participants in this most recent study did cite historical or literary figures and used this identification with historical figures as their real-time muse. Some even talked directly to their muse, asking questions such as, "What would Queen Elizabeth do in this situation?" or "How would Nancy Drew solve that problem?"

Other participants I interviewed told me they wanted a more direct connection to their muse. In these cases, the participants created a physical representation on paper of their preferred leadership components (or montage) so that their visualization was more tangible and directly actionable.

> *The entire complex of our consciousness develops largely by absorbing parts of meaningful people in our lives...We do not become the people from whom we learn any more than we become the food we eat, but an aspect of them does become a part of us.*
>
> —Arthur and Libby Coleman

My consulting and coaching practice also was a source of refining the concepts in this book as are formal focus groups I conducted with emerging leaders.

The young leader cited earlier in this chapter, Ashley, decided to take this direct illustrative path and graphically demonstrated how the influences of certain leaders had supported her leadership journey (see Figure 1.1 following page). Creating such representations is not required in the role montage process, but many of those I've coached through the process find such tactile representations help them visualize the new path they want to follow.

But no matter how such personal discoveries are expressed, the leaders I interviewed found their discoveries valuable in the same way that researchers Arthur and Libby Coleman found to be true in the sidebar quote about the visualization process—that we do indeed "absorb" aspects of those we admire into our lives and that they ultimately become "part of us."[3]

ROLE MONTAGE, A TOOL FOR SELF-AWARENESS

Role montage exploration is a potent practice for generating self-awareness. It fulfills an internal longing to make meaning out of all our life's experiences. The fictional characters and real people we encounter during our lives are part of this rich pattern of influences. In the example of Ashley, we see someone who is using role montage as a self-awareness tool to discover her leadership gaps and what she needs to do to help her team.

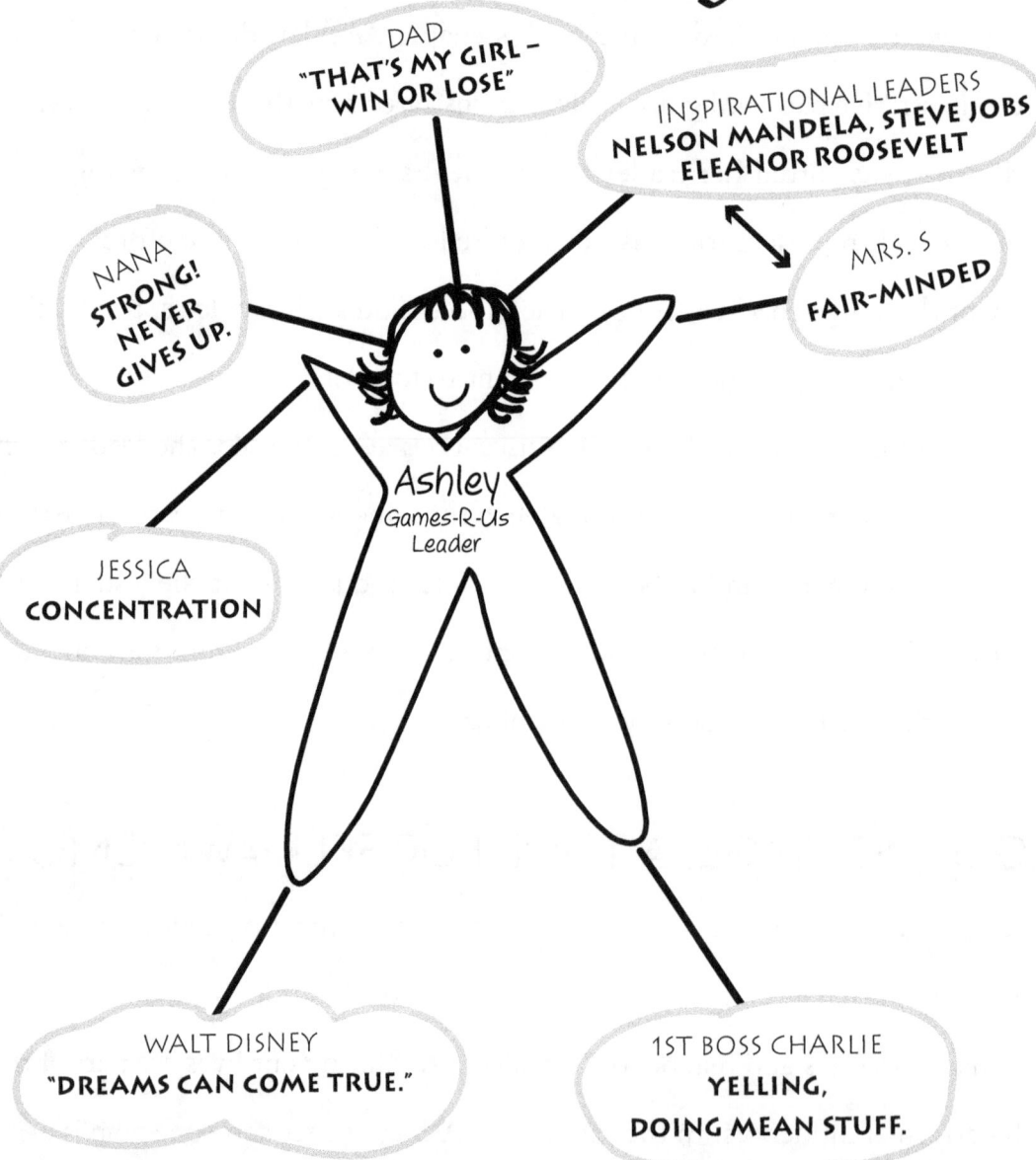

If Ashley made a role montage, it might look like this.

FIGURE 1.1

ROLE MONTAGE, A DIAGNOSTIC TOOL

Role montage exploration also can be used as a diagnostic tool for those who don't have time to participate in a 360-degree feedback process or other self-assessment instruments. By examining people of influence and identifying the ones you'd want to emulate, a picture is created that allows you to develop a plan for self-improvement and career success. Here's an example from my own consulting practice.

Rufus, a mid-level executive at XYZ Biometrics, wanted to establish a career development plan but had never taken the time to do it. I coached him to look at his mentors and role models and suggested he write down the qualities that most influenced him and the ones that he wanted to embody. He examined both the leaders he admired and those he didn't. His list of mentors and role models was wide ranging and even included sports figures. Once he carefully examined his list of characteristics he discovered that he needed to work on delegation to be a more effective leader. With this knowledge, we created a plan to help him develop this vital leadership skill.

CONCLUSION

In changing and turbulent times, it is important to have a map of where you want to take your leadership. Role montage is a creative new way to see the patterns and develop a collage of the most important influences in your life. It builds your self-awareness and helps to discover the leader within you.

The exercises at the end of the chapter will help you analyze your own leadership, mentors, role models, and the qualities you need to develop your leadership capabilities. These exercises will also help build self-awareness and are critical foundational elements that will help you create your own powerful role montage.

Chapter 1 Exercises

Getting Started

Exploration is a potent practice in role montage because it fulfills an internal longing to make meaning out of the fictional or real characters we read or hear about in addition to the people we meet along our life's pathway. Successful leaders must develop a keen sense of self-awareness. Such self-awareness is critical to building new behaviors and new skills. The exercises that follow will help you identify the people and characters who inspire you toward reaching your potential as a leader.

Exercise A

Consider the full landscape of the people (family, fictional characters, famous athletes, entertainers, etc.) you've encountered in your life. It's a lot to contemplate, but it is an essential reflection to tackle. Don't worry about leaving out someone or an important experience right now. You can return to this exercise later if you wish. What's most important is that you begin the process of identifying these essential influences. You can also download the worksheets used throughout this book on the associated website www.rolemontage.com.

Exercise B

Consider the list of influences you made in Exercise A. Take some time to reflect about these people and the impact they had on your journey toward becoming an effective leader. As you contemplate the traits you admire, make a notation as to whether or not you share these qualities or if there is a deficit you want to fill.

This will help you form a development plan for the future. It will show areas where you need to find additional mentors, role models, coaches, and other resources. Note that it is equally important to pay attention to the qualities you don't want to emulate.

Examine what you can learn from the negative qualities of these people. Give the questions below serious consideration and jot down the answers either in this book or use the online forms available at www.rolemontage.com.

CHAPTER 1

Finding Your Inspiration

A. WHO HAS INFLUENCED YOU?

_____

_____

What qualities do you admire about these people?

_____

_____

What qualities do you want to emulate?

_____

_____

What are the negative qualities they might have?

_____

_____

B. WHAT QUALITIES DO YOU SHARE WITH YOUR ROLE MONTAGE CHOICES?

_____

_____

How can you develop the qualities that you don't share with them?

_____

_____

How will these qualities move you toward your leadership goals?

_____

_____

Chapter 2
SELF-AWARENESS AND THE SUCCESSFUL LEADER

In This Chapter

- Definition of Self-Awareness
- What Makes a Successful Leader?
- Developing Self-Awareness
- A Personal Mentor Example
- Links to Emotional Intelligence
- How Self-Awareness Impacts Leadership
- Conclusion
- Chapter 2 Exercises

Developing self-awareness is not always an easy path for leaders to follow. Many find objectively exploring personal motivation in a deep and meaningful way difficult to achieve. Yet, without this self-awareness exploration, building trust and credibility is a burdensome, if not an impossible task.[4] As the sidebar quote by organizational leadership consultant Warren Bennis makes clear, self-awareness goes beyond how we conduct ourselves in the workplace. Self-awareness is at the core of becoming a fully integrated human being.

> *The process of becoming a leader is similar, if not identical, to becoming a fully integrated human being… {and both are} grounded in self-discovery.*
>
> —Warren Bennis

Here's a story taken from my leadership study about Keisha that highlights this point. As the leader of a conflict resolution group in an inner-city neighborhood, understanding her motivations was essential to her own leadership journey.

> *My job is very stimulating and stressful at the same time, because there are lots of disagreements and prolonged fighting in the neighborhood. I understand that a good leader is self-aware, but I cannot afford the time or expense to engage a therapist or a coach to help me on my journey. Instead, I've gained self-knowledge through introspection after*

soliciting feedback from my team, the people I manage, and from my closest friends.

Although hearing critical or negative feedback is difficult, I persisted through the difficult process. I eventually learned that my team and those I manage perceived me to be a micro-manager. Instead of becoming defensive, I chose to examine the feedback and determine what I could do to change this behavior.

Keisha told me her change process was slow at first. She began by simply refraining from always questioning the work or results of her team or of those she managed. She stopped hovering over her staff and carefully watching over their work. She actively supported this behavior change by reading management and leadership books to support and improve these essential skills.

Soon, Keisha told me, the same feedback loop that had told her she was a micromanager let her know that her leadership style was building credibility and trust among her team members and those she managed.

The story of Anya, a newly hired human resources vice president at a large school district, is another example of how putting in place a simple self-awareness feedback process can bring positive change:

I have my team's back and they have mine. We didn't always have this kind of relationship. I got feedback from my team and from my peers that the person who held the job before me used to take credit for everyone's work. He didn't do a good job of protecting the team from the executive group, and he rarely supported them.

It's taken me a couple of months to win the respect and confidence of my team. I frequently check-in to get feedback on how I'm doing and how we are working as a team. I was pleased to find a consensus that we were a much more cohesive group.

In addition to this feedback loop, I gained self-awareness and confidence in myself through introspection and meditation. My meditation teacher provided helpful behaviors to practice when my job is too stressful. He taught me to, "center, align, and ground" myself. I practice this mantra almost every day and especially when I'm confronted with hostile situations such as an angry employee, parent or student.

DEFINITION OF SELF-AWARENESS

Self-awareness is the capacity to know or to understand one's self and includes the desire to learn more about one's own behaviors, thought patterns, and emotions. It's also an ability to evaluate how others perceive us and to make necessary changes through authentic feedback and reflection.

WHAT MAKES A SUCCESSFUL LEADER?

As American essayist Ralph Waldo Emerson says in the sidebar quote, successful leadership is one part enthusiasm and one part self-awareness.

Kathy, a participant in one of my studies, and the top executive at a school with challenging students, described successful leadership by using a metaphor of "ballroom dancing."

> *Leading people is like a dance. You have to bring your partner along and be sensitive to where they are so you don't step on their toes. If you are leading, then you need to be aware of whether or not you are in tune with the other person or why you are not.*

Clearly, Kathy, who was an experienced leader, had a keen understanding of what it takes to be an effective leader.

Madison, an executive director of a growing nonprofit organization, and one of the youngest participants in my study, provided another excellent description of a leadership path. Here's

---

Enthusiasm is one of the most powerful engines of success. When you do a thing, do it with all your might. Put your whole soul into it. Stamp it with your own personality. Be active, be energetic, be enthusiastic and faithful, and you will accomplish your objective. Nothing great was ever achieved without enthusiasm.

—Ralph Waldo Emerson

how Madison framed her own introspective journey: "Self-awareness is a journey. It's messy and complex and it takes time and practice."

DEVELOPING SELF-AWARENESS

Leaders use a variety of methods to build self-awareness, but as Kathy notes success depends on being highly motivated, taking an appropriate amount of time and finding the psychic space necessary to create a supportive environment for the process of change. You'll find an exercise at the end of this chapter that will give some clarity on your strengths and what's important to you. Some people choose a more introspective way to become more self-aware and use meditation and reflection practices; others choose to use a role montage practice.

One of my coaching clients at a high-technology company in Beijing was enthusiastic and ambitious. She clearly had a supportive environment as the company required its leaders to have external coaches and internal mentors to help them develop their self-awareness and upgrade their behavioral skills.

Here's how the client, Li Chen, approached her self-awareness journey and specifically through the use of role montage.

> *Li Chen wanted to improve her facilitation skills and sought feedback from both her team and her boss. She learned that her lack of self-confidence was impacting her performance, so her supervisor suggested that Li Chen begin*

the change process by developing her self-awareness through meditation and listening to her own "inner voice."

At the same time, Li Chen began a mentoring relationship with a company vice-president, a woman she very much admired, who was also an excellent facilitator. The work she did with the vice president greatly increased her self-awareness and confidence.

My role montage work with Li Chen helped her further develop these positive qualities. While her mentor was a key part of her final role montage, Li Chen's grandmother was an even larger influence on her life and thus a larger part of her role montage. In fact, she remembered her grandmother telling her on a number of occasions, "Knowing others is intelligence. Knowing yourself is true wisdom (Lao Tzu)." Li Chen also included her highly supportive uncle in the role montage she eventually created. Figure 2.1 is the graphic version of her role montage.

Li Chen's role models and mentors encouraged her skills, helped her build her self-awareness, and contributed to her ultimate success. A significant part of Li Chen's success was the simple act of observing others being successful in a role and then emulating and ultimately "taking on board" the characteristics of others through her use of role montage.

Some aspiring leaders might have difficulty locating role models with similar backgrounds and experiences inside their organizations. One of my participants

Role Montage

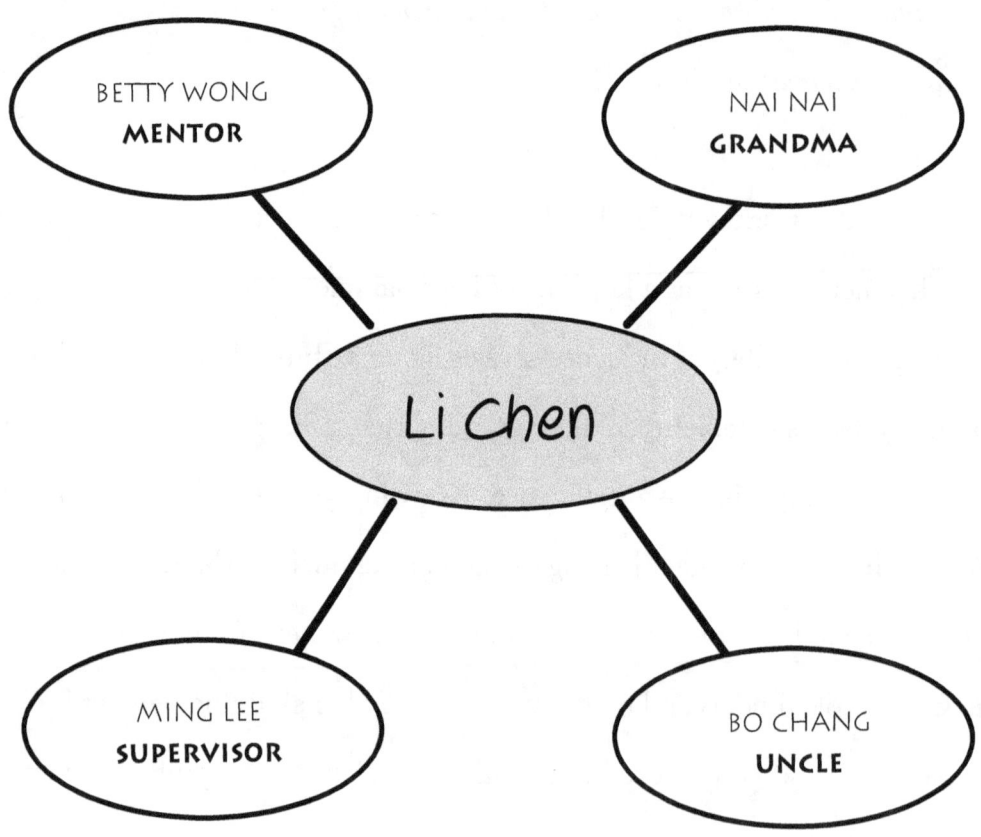

FIGURE 2.1

actively searched for women who had achieved success in her organizations and who showed evidence of the kind of self-awareness that led them on their journeys up the corporate ladder. After conducting the leadership interviews, I realized how significant it was to have real role models (this is especially true for women as suggested by the sidebar quote from Meryl Streep).

> *It is not a simple job to be a role model. It is not just being endlessly compassionate, polite, and well groomed. It's equal parts being who you actually are, and what people hope you will be. It's representing for all women to be our best selves.*
>
> —Meryl Streep

As these women leaders move upward in their organizations, they need role models who can help these aspiring women visualize being effective using behaviors that might be different from those they observe in men. Here is what Suzanne, a finance director at a biotechnology company, told me about the importance of observing the success of others:

> *I watched the dynamics of how my manager, another woman, influenced others, because she was smart, knew a lot about business, and was politically savvy. I observed the way she worked and how she was respected, because what's tolerated and expected for women managers is different from men.*
>
> *If women are firm, they can be viewed as harsh, difficult, or a bitch. Having a role model {who knows how to walk this thin line} was a key component for my success.*

All these leaders in the previous examples used feedback either through introspection (as Keisha did) or through the meditative practice (as the Anya example demonstrates) or direct observation as evidenced by Suzanne's story.

Once you've acquired these skills, then you'll be able to take on the intellectual, physical, and emotional challenges of leadership that require you to "regularly step into the inner chamber of your being and assess the tolls those challenges are taking"[5] as leadership authorities Ronald Heifetz and Marty Linsky describe the internal process of leadership. It is essential work for all leaders. Those who don't take the time for this self-exploration pay the cost through missed opportunities and poor results. Here's a story that illustrates this dynamic.

Vivienne, a Millennial leader of a nonprofit organization for battered women, is observant about the people around her. She belongs to a support group of nonprofit leaders who mentor one another. According to Vivienne, the results are not good when leaders don't access their inner chambers of self-awareness.

> *When I see leaders who are not self-aware, it scares me because their management breaks down. It's difficult to get things done, and they have poor relationships with their Boards. I observed this behavior with one of our support group members. Rhys seemed to have little self-awareness. He likes to tell his Board that he's completed certain tasks even when he knows he can't meet their requirements. He doesn't want to disappoint them.*

> *He has little confidence in himself and hardly any self-awareness. Rhys is unable to delegate to staff, because their funding is quite limited and the staff comes in only part-time to do their jobs and not to do extra work. Rhys' management was breaking down. Eventually, the team was demoralized until most of the staff started looking for other jobs.*

Clearly, this poor leadership situation, fueled by lack of confidence and self-awareness directly impacts the team's performance and the viability of the organization. For emerging leaders, developing self-awareness helps them become comfortable as leaders and assists in the growth of their intuition and problem-solving abilities. Finding a mentor, role model, exploring role montage techniques, or even learning meditation or reflection practices can assist in achieving the necessary leadership self-awareness.

A PERSONAL MENTOR EXAMPLE

My mentor and role model, Edie Seashore,[6] told me many stories that were humorous and meaningful and often came with a punch-line message. The story of how we met has had a great impact on me.

> *Edie and I met at a conference in the late 1970s where she and two male colleagues were leading a popular workshop on men and women's communication. One of her colleagues was at the front of the room asking the 150*

participants in the room to arrange themselves into small groups. No one moved. Everyone kept on talking to one another.

Edie walked from the back of the room, down the center aisle, and said with conviction, "I want you to get into small groups NOW!" Every person in the room jumped and got into a small group.

Edie and I discussed what happened at this conference and why her direct, forceful approach had worked. Edie said the participants moved because she "believed they would {move}." The idea that my "belief" in the outcome influences what ultimately happens has gotten me through many professional and personal challenges. I always say to myself, "I believe they will…I believe I can."

Edie was a pioneer in the field of women and work—an inspiration for me when she consulted to the US Naval Academy during their integration of women into the school. I brought Edie to a company conference as the keynote speaker when I worked in the Silicon Valley. She stirred the all-male executive team with her stories of sexual harassment at the Academy so much so that after her presentation the company changed its sexual harassment approach in a fundamental way.

Edie Seashore is certainly part of my role montage. When I think deeply or draw an image of my role montage, Edie is a prominent part of it. Her particular example has been very helpful to me throughout the years, and it has changed how I approach both my work and personal life.

LINKS TO EMOTIONAL INTELLIGENCE

Self-awareness is an essential part of emotional intelligence. The studies on emotional intelligence by psychologist Daniel Goleman show self-awareness as the first component of emotional intelligence (EI) at work:[7]

- **Self-awareness**—the ability to know one's emotions, strengths, weaknesses, values and goals and recognize their impact on others while using gut feelings to guide decisions.

- **Self-regulation**—involves controlling or redirecting one's disruptive emotions and impulses and adapting to changing circumstances.

- **Social skill**—managing relationships to move people in the desired direction.

- **Empathy**—considering other people's feelings especially when making decisions.

- **Motivation**—being driven to achieve for the sake of achievement.

Goleman's model, as shown above, focuses on emotional intelligence as a wide array of competencies and skills that drive leadership performance. According to Goleman, emotional competencies are not innate talents, but rather learned capabilities that can be developed to achieve outstanding performance. Goleman says that emotional self-awareness consists of the "ability to read and understand your emotions as well as recognize their impact on work performance, relationships, and the like."[8]

The history of "emotional intelligence" came originally from the research of developmental psychologist Howard Gardner, whose book[9] in the early 1980s posited the idea that traditional types of intelligence, such as IQ, fail to fully explain cognitive ability, and he introduced the idea of multiple intelligences.

In the late 1980s, John Mayer and Peter Salovey, two psychologists, offered the first formulation of a concept they called "emotional intelligence." The construct first appeared in the literature in 1990 when they published an article titled "Emotional Intelligence"[10] that explained an organizing theory of the abilities they believed at the time would be adaptive in thinking about, and thinking with, emotions. Goleman saw this article as a science writer for the *New York Times*, and made some changes to their theory that he discusses in his widely popular book.[11]

As Goleman explains, leaders become more aware of their own strengths and the opportunities for development when they seek honest feedback. Leaders in my study reported that self-awareness affected their leadership in a number of positive ways in addition to making them more aware of how their behavior affected other people. They were able to empower their teams and "lead from the center" based on the feedback results they received and were able to build trust throughout their organizations.

Appendix D has three feedback forms: a form to list the people you want to ask to give you feedback; an email to send to the participants once you have chosen them; and a brief feedback survey that you can use to obtain feedback information about your behavior.

Hannah, president at a bank, started as a teller, told me that self-awareness was essential to her reaching the pinnacle of her career.

I don't think you can be an effective leader without self-awareness. You have to have high EQ [emotional intelligence]. You have to be accountable for what you're doing, learning more about yourself, and using the feedback you receive to make the necessary changes.

Self-awareness is part of emotional intelligence and helps people recognize their patterns of behavior and how it impacts their relationships. For existing leaders, strengthening self-awareness practices can improve one's effectiveness in other areas of leadership, such as understanding corporate culture, working more effectively with teams, building relationships, and thinking more strategically.

HOW SELF-AWARENESS IMPACTS LEADERSHIP

Leaders in my study reported that self-awareness affected their leadership in positive ways. They became more aware of their strengths and the opportunities for development by asking for feedback that in turn led to more self-understanding. One of the positive ways included making them more aware of how their behavior affected other people. They were in alignment with their teams and built trust with them.

An example of this behavior is Mia, an academic leader in a middle school, where she always tries to improve herself and her team.

> *I like getting into things I haven't been exposed to before, and especially learning new concepts. I'm always aware of how my behavior affects my team and those around us. I believe leadership is an ability to do things and make them happen by creating an environment of trust and confidence.*
>
> *I believe that self-awareness is a key component to my success. I learn from people I trust, and I ask them for feedback. I see feedback as an area for growth, self-understanding and a place to improve. I like to have people on my team who think in a different way than I do or the rest of the staff so it stretches all of us.*

Mia has a successful team who likes to follow her because she has good relationships with her manager and other supervisors and with her own team members. She listens to her team's needs, wants, and desires, and she takes their feedback to heart.

Some key impacts of self-awareness on leadership from the leaders in my study are:

- Greater awareness of others' behavior and emotions

- Discovery of strengths

- Importance of building relationships

- Able to hear difficult feedback and be responsive to it

- Improved communication

- Greater emotional intelligence

CONCLUSION

Developing self-awareness is a key factor in successful and effective leadership. Satisfied leaders realize that insight and self-knowledge are important competencies for reaching high-level goals. The leaders in my study suggested an introspective path to achieving self-awareness. They were able to harness self-awareness for increasing their productiveness and understanding their true potential. Self-awareness creates trust and credibility for leaders and the people who work with them. Self-aware leaders with high emotional intelligence access their power and use it to create more positive change globally.

Chapter 2 Exercises

Getting Started

The three exercises that follow will help you grow your self-understanding and assist you in identifying the people and characters that inspire you to reach your potential as a leader.

Exercise A

Developing self-awareness is a key factor in successful and effective leadership. Think about times when you learned about yourself—your strengths, areas of growth, communication styles, and leadership. Then you can ask for feedback from your staff, peers, or those you feel comfortable with, including friends.

Think about the leadership qualities that you possess and any mentors who might be able to give you an unbiased view of your strengths and challenges. See Appendix D for a Request for Feedback Form. It can be difficult to ask others for feedback, so review the form in Appendix D. You can jot down the answers either in this book or use the online form available at www.rolemontage.com.

Exercise B

Self-awareness creates trust and credibility with leaders and the people who work with them. My participants suggested an introspective path to achieving self-awareness. Small amounts or lack of self-awareness have a detrimental effect on the leaders themselves and also on their teams.

In Exercise B, list those who helped to develop your self-awareness and the messages that you received from them. Think about how those messages impacted you. The personal example I gave of Edie Seashore mentions a message that I received from her that changed my life. How have the messages or stories that you got changed you?

 ## Exercise C

Consider the list you made of people and messages that have influenced and inspired you in Exercise B. Take some time to consider how these people and experiences have helped you know more about yourself and how those dynamics changed your behavior at work and at home. Your greater self-knowledge will benefit those you manage and help you on your journey toward becoming a better leader. You may jot down the answers either in this book or use the online form available at www.rolemontage.com.

Building Self-Awareness

EXERCISE A

1. List your strengths.

   _____

   _____

   _____

2. List your areas for growth.

   _____

   _____

   _____

3. What is your communication and leadership style?

   _____

   _____

   _____

EXERCISE B

1. Who helped you to develop your self-awareness?

   _____

2. When were the times you learned about yourself?

   List names below of those who developed and inspired you.

   _____

3. What messages did you learn from the times you learned about yourself?

   _____

4. What messages did you receive from those who helped develop your self-awareness?

   _____

5. How did these messages boost your self-awareness?

   _____

6. What insight did it give to you?

   _____

EXERCISE C

1. What do you now know about yourself?

   _____

2. How has that changed your behavior at work or at home?

   _____

3. Consider your responses above and take some time to think about how you intend to implement the changes you are seeking to make.

   _____

4. Changes I Intend to Make

   _____

5. How Will I Implement These Changes?

   _____

Chapter 3
THE ROLE MONTAGE ADVANTAGE

In This Chapter

- Role Montage Example
- Personal Example
- Negative People in Role Montage
- Why Role Montage Is a Powerful Tool
- Few Role Models for Women
- Conclusion
- Chapter 3 Exercises

> *Be ready to learn throughout your entire life and to observe reality in yourself and in the world at all times.*
>
> —Thích Nhất Hạnh

Role montage is a structured way to use our mostly hidden expressive and artistic abilities to become more self-aware and to improve our decision-making and leadership abilities. The process is similar to artistic montage work in that both are created from an assemblage of different impressions superimposed on one another and blended in such a way that allows each individual piece to remain distinct. It's a way of living and learning about ourselves that is perfectly captured by the Thích Nhất Hạnh sidebar quote.

Existing leaders like the role montage process because it helps them identify viable role models and provides support when looking for solutions to difficult problems. Emerging leaders find role montage a useful tool for understanding the influencers of their leadership style and to identify which leaders to engage with (or visualize engaging with) to help them continue their learning journey.

ROLE MONTAGE EXAMPLE

In many ways, role montage is the assemblage of various people who advise us (serve as our mentors); who we imitate (become our role models); and who inspire us (become our heroes and heroines). These influencers are all blended into artwork and used as internal guidance for our leadership journey.

Both real people and imaginary characters form the basis of this artwork as the example of Rachel, an executive director for a social justice nonprofit and blogger, demonstrates. Rachel used the montage process to surface those who influenced her journey toward becoming an executive director (see Figure 3.1 next page).

I was surrounded by strong women growing up (my mom, my aunt, my grandmother, and my older sister). My mom taught me to read when I was four years old. I love to read, and some of the most important aspects of my montage come from books. One of my favorite characters is Atticus Finch in **To Kill a Mockingbird**, *because he courageously supported outcasts and victims of prejudice as I do in my current work.*

My high school English lit teacher, Ms. Martine, recognized some promise in me and was always trying to stretch me. She made me editor of the newspaper, and I strove to push myself further because of her influence.

The women leaders in my study liked the idea of role montage exploration because they didn't often have women as role models. They used the process to gain access to their internal influencer map. Some leaders chose real people as influencers; for example, Eleanor Roosevelt, Maya Angelou, Georgia O'Keeffe, David Sedaris, and even their parents. Others chose imaginary characters like Lulu (of comic strip fame) and Buzz Lightyear (from the movie *Toy Story*). Who (or what) these influencers are is not as important as the way you internalize them to build your role montage.

Role Montage

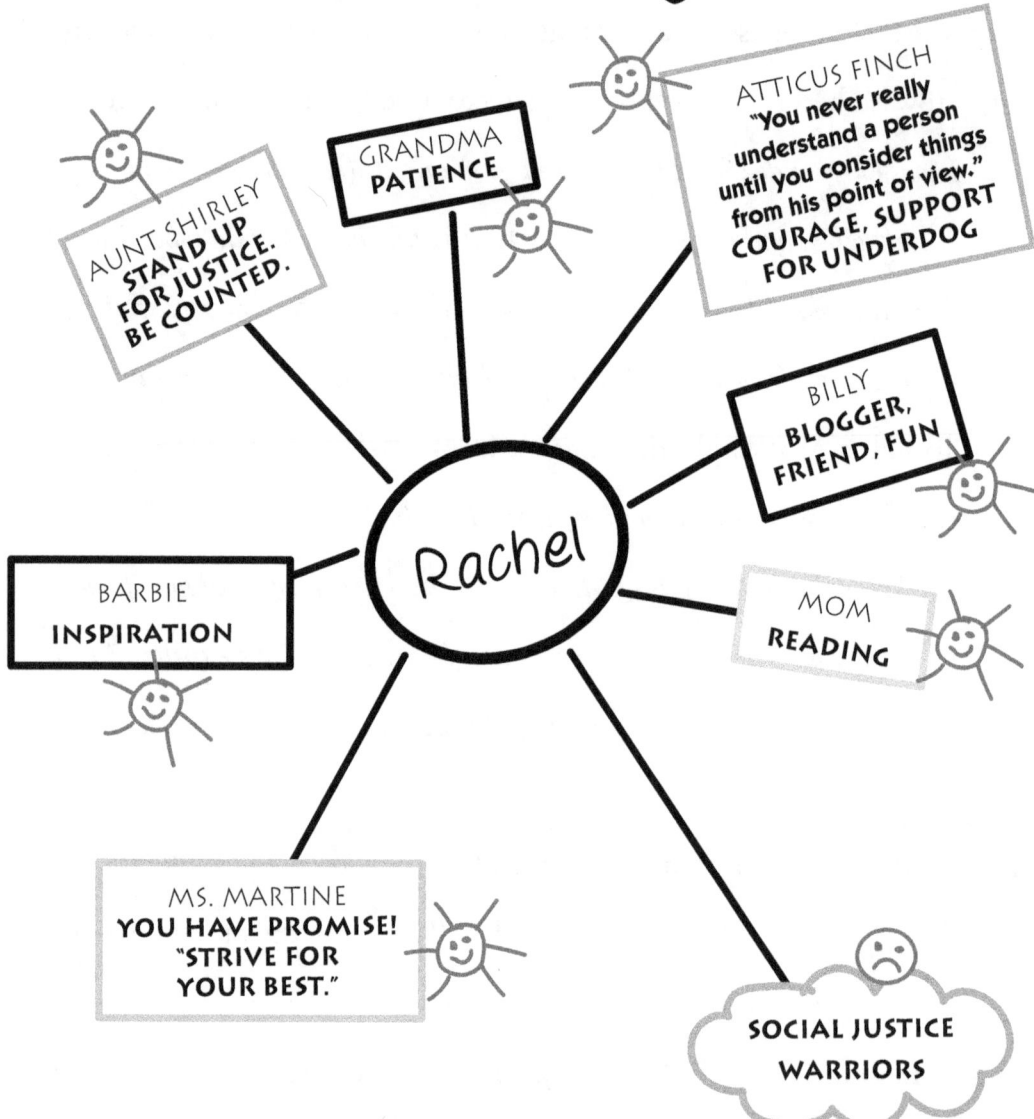

Rachel, Executive Director of Social Justice
Also a Blogger

FIGURE 3.1

PERSONAL EXAMPLE

Role montage opens your eyes to new perspectives and assists you in recognizing your patterns of thinking and feeling and to discover the basis of your values. For example, when I worked twelve-hour days at a high-technology company in the Silicon Valley, I drew on the strength I found in my own montage. Here's my story:

When I was struggling and discouraged from my long commute and feeling that I wasn't doing such a good job, I remembered my Aunt Vicky. She always made me feel worthwhile and loved me unconditionally especially when I was a teenager and having problems with my own mom.

As I faced problems at work, my thoughts turned to Aunt Vicky and the faith that she had in me. Even though she worked long hours, she took me under her wing, because family always came first.

Edie Seashore (mentioned in an earlier chapter) is another example of a mentor who is part of my montage. Edie consulted with clients all over the world, but when her daughters were teenagers and needed her, Edie moved her consulting practice back to the Washington, DC, area to be close to them. I followed Edie's example when my own children were in high school. I left my work in the Silicon Valley for private practice so that I'd be home when my kids got home from school. Role montage allows us to take parts or qualities of people we admire and internalize these attributes and make them our own.

NEGATIVE PEOPLE IN ROLE MONTAGE

You probably know a number of people with negative behaviors that you wouldn't want to emulate or perhaps you know a leader with a style of leadership you believe to be ineffective. While you might respect some aspect of a leader's style or the positive attributes of someone you know, you are still wary of including them in your role montage unless you focus only on the positive.

Rhiannon, a leader at a consulting firm, had a similar situation with a leader she wanted to include in her role montage. She admired the company's vice president's ability to set boundaries, in particular the vice president's ability to leave work every day in time to pick up her children. Rhiannon had a new baby and so leaving work on time was of particular importance to her.

However, the vice president had some negative leadership attributes that Rhiannon definitely did not want to mirror, specifically a tendency to be punitive and authoritarian with her management team. In Rhiannon's case she had to be clear in her intentions by saying to herself, "that's not the kind of leader I want to be."

Like Rhiannon, most of us base a lot of our leadership style on what we observe in others. Unfortunately, sometimes we lack positive experiences with a competent leader. You're ahead of the game if you can separate the good from the bad as Rhiannon did with the leader she wanted to include in her role montage.

All of us possess skills, strengths, and talents in addition to flaws and perhaps some negative behaviors. The exercises that you completed at the end of Chapter

1 helped you identify who influenced you in both positive and negative ways. The exercises at the end of Chapter 2 helped you identify your strengths and areas for development and growth. What is important is to know how to balance the positive and negative in the role montage you ultimately create.

WHY ROLE MONTAGE IS A POWERFUL TOOL

Creating a personal role montage enables you to create an internalized picture of your best self and become a grounded, fully realized leader (a whole human being). Role montage focuses your attention on integrating the influences of your most powerful real or imagined role model, mentor, hero, and heroine. It's an exploration that helps find connection and mirrors the successful style and characteristics of those we admire. Listed in the box are the advantages of role montage and why it's such a powerful tool.

Advantages of a Role Montage

- Helps find connections and mirrors successful style of leaders we admire.
- Offers a broader definition that includes more aspects of personality.
- Assists in making sense of our role models, mentors, memories, dreams, and reflections.
- Fills a gap for those without mentors and role models.
- Creates a powerful way to learn self-awareness.

One of the leaders in my study, Sara, found great advantage in role montage when she discovered her underlying fear of speaking in front of large groups of people. This fear came to the surface when she got the top job at a large, national organization.

> *I was terrified to speak in front of large groups of people especially since the former CEO was an excellent speaker and storyteller. She was a hard act to follow. I realized that I had to do something about it. Usually I read books to help me with my management style.*
>
> *Somehow I didn't think that would help in this situation. I finally asked the previous CEO how she did it. She told me to watch myself in front of a mirror giving a speech and to hire a speech coach. That help made all the difference.*

As part of her role montage practice, Sara paid attention to the most important figures in her montage, which included the former CEO of her company. She also sought out the advice of other leaders who were excellent speakers. All this direct input turned out to be a powerful way for Sara to learn about herself and grow as a confident speaker and leader.

Another participant, Isabella, had little confidence in herself because she lacked a college degree. Her manager was a division vice president of a large company and she thought Isabella was an excellent contributor. Isabella and I explored her role montage possibilities together and as her confidence began to grow she was able to accept an invitation from her manager to become her running partner.

During the next few months, Isabella and her manager ran every day at lunch and eventually Isabella competed in a marathon, a feat that was a big confidence booster for Isabella. She was able to achieve this difficult goal in part due to her role montage work and the successful images she had internalized that included her role models, mentors, and historical figures she admired—and even a few cartoon characters. We all have these powerful role montages within us, even if we are not consciously aware of it. By exploring your montage, you get in touch with important positive messages that influence your behavior and choices and eventually open doors to new possibilities.

Another client, Michael, told me that Sir Laurence Olivier was part of his role montage because Olivier was known to get sick with fear before he went on stage. Yet he went on stage anyway. Michael said that he admired Olivier for his forthrightness in telling the truth about this debilitating nervousness. Michael told me that Olivier's experiences had helped him through many rough moments in his career, especially when he had to defend his work performance.

FEW ROLE MODELS FOR WOMEN

Christine Lagarde, who is chair of one of the world's largest law firms and, since 2011, head of the International Monetary Fund, in 2000 said, "Don't imitate what the guys do…Women bring different things to the table from what men generally bring."[12] Lagarde is right. Women should expect to have other women to set examples for them. Liz, a Millennial in my study who was at an early stage in her career and just starting her own consulting firm, told me "I found it very interesting to tell my story to you and what struck me the most was the realization that I don't have role models or mentors, so your dissertation concept, role montage, is dead on." This lack of role models is especially true for women of color who have even fewer opportunities for growth and development inside their organizations.

Technology executive Sheryl Sandberg, in her book *Lean In: Women, Work, and the Will to Lead*, put the onus on both men and women to fix organizations. Sandberg suggests that men and women need to change this restrictive system. The first step is to be aware of the bias, have conversations about it and then be motivated to correct it. Organizations can benefit by encouraging the discussions because both men and women will benefit from making attitudinal shifts that allow them to be more authentic in the workplace.[13]

CONCLUSION

Role montage encourages the internal process of uniting the diverse parts of ourselves by filling in gaps that make up our complex multidimensional identity. Women and men seeking powerful positions in organizations can use role montage to build these essential inner images of themselves. By naming and mapping your inspirational influences, you can understand who has had the most impact on your life and use this knowledge as a potent way to examine your own leadership potential.

Chapter 3 Exercises

Getting Started

Change is always a difficult process. This is especially true when you are working on adjusting lifelong habits and beliefs. To grow self-awareness, you have to be willing to step into the unknown and be vulnerable. This is especially true when getting feedback. I always advise clients to make themselves vulnerable and report back to the people who offered feedback. As scary as it seems, it's one of the most rewarding activities you can do. The following exercises will help you examine your motivation and commitment to make changes in your life.

Exercise A

Exploration is a potent practice in role montage work because it fulfills an internal longing to make meaning out of real or fictional characters and people you meet during your life's journeys. Successful leaders must develop a keen sense of self-awareness so that they can connect to their deepest values and then make necessary changes to create new behaviors and build new skills. This exercise will help you determine your readiness for role montage work. Give the questions below serious consideration and jot down the answers either in this book or use the online form available at www.rolemontage.com.

Exercise B

This exercise asks you to rate your willingness to make the changes on a scale of 0 to 10 considering what you stated in Exercise A. Ten is the most willing, and 0 is not willing at all to change. Circle the change willingness factor and explain your answer in the space provided.

Exercise C

Consider how you have reacted to change in the past. What assisted you in making changes? Take your time to consider the idea of change and how it affects you and how you respond to it.

CHAPTER 3

Are You Ready for Role Montage?

EXERCISE A

What changes would you like manifested?

_____

How would you identify them on a role montage?

_____

What habits or tendencies might stand in your way to your development?

_____

How would you identify them on a role montage?

_____

What might help you overcome these roadblocks to change?

_____

EXERCISE B

Circle the number that most closely represents your willingness to change.

Unwilling to Change   Completely Willing to Change

0   1   2   3   4   5   6   7   8   9   10

Explain Your Answer

_____

_____

EXERCISE C

Consider your responses above and take some time to think about how you intend to implement the changes you are seeking to make.

Change I Intend to Make

_____

How I Will Implement this Change

_____

Chapter 4
HOW TO DESIGN A ROLE MONTAGE

In This Chapter

- Starting a Role Montage
- Instructions for Completing a Role Montage
- Questions to Consider
- Mapping Guide
- What to Do Next
- Conclusion
- Chapter 4 Exercises

> *In collage...You first of all draw it on the paper, then you cut it up, then you paste it down, then you change it, then you shove it about, then you may paint bits of it over, so actually you're not making the picture there and then, you're making it through a process, so it's not so spontaneous.*
>
> —Paula Rego

A role montage is designed in a similar way to an art montage. The former is created from an assemblage of different people who have influenced you, while the latter is made from art pieces superimposed one on another over time, so that they form a blended whole while remaining distinct. Paula Rego, a Portuguese visual artist, explains in the sidebar quote the process she uses to create a collage. It takes time and is not a spontaneous, short-term process.

If you complete the exercises at the end of the previous chapters and follow the steps in this chapter, you will have created a good role montage exploration process that will be useful in your self-awareness journey.

STARTING A ROLE MONTAGE

Role montage exploration has a powerful effect on your identity and is a definite boost to your career and personal life. The role montage process itself will help identify the influential figures that reinforce the leadership behaviors you strive for and will support your plan for self-improvement.

The role montage work can help identify and enhance missing behaviors and skills. This aspect of role montage is especially true if the process helps you discover that none of your major influencers have the particular leadership qualities you want to develop. If this is the case, then you'll need to find other means for obtaining these qualities, such as new mentors, training classes, or workshops, to name a few.

INSTRUCTIONS FOR COMPLETING A ROLE MONTAGE[14]

Here are three ways to begin working on your montage. The **first** is to simply dive in immediately and make a list of the people who might fit with the role montage you imagine creating. Once the list is made, you begin the design process as Rachel did in Chapter 3. In Rachel's case she knew who the influencers were in her life so the inspiration discovery process was less structured, and she didn't need to answer questions listed in this chapter.

The **second** way, if you are not sure of the list of people, as was the case with some of the young, emerging leaders in my focus groups, is to answer the questions featured in the next section of this chapter. It will be a helpful, and often fun, tool to move forward in the process.

The **third** path is to review examples of the role montage work others have completed. I provide some examples at the end of this chapter. Some are hand drawn—my preference—and others are done on a computer. You also can use magazine pictures to create your montage. There are examples at the end of the chapter. All of these approaches are fine, so let your learning style guide what works best for you. My own montages are in Appendix C at the end of the book.

QUESTIONS TO CONSIDER

Use the questions below to guide the development of your personal list of people and characters who support your leadership journey. When you choose an influencer, include the inspirational qualities they possess and any quotes of inspiration associated with the figure if possible. Remember to include any appropriate messages, metaphors, or stories that are relevant to your journey.

You may answer the questions now or wait until the end of the chapter, but in either case pay particular attention to the last question, as most of my clients find this question to be the one that is most revealing and creative.

- Who in my family influenced me and why?

- What teachers made a difference for me and why? (preschool, elementary, middle, high school, college)

- Who are my favorite entertainers on television, in movies, and in the music scene?

- Who is my favorite artist, cartoonist, author, or blogger?

- What character in a book do I identify with the most?

- What manager or team leader influenced me the most?

- What world leaders or historical persons influenced me?

- What qualities or attributes did I admire about all of them?

- Are there any negative role models who illuminate other aspects of my montage that I want to be aware of?

- Who supported and recognized my leadership the most? When and how did they do so?

- If you could invite anyone, living or dead, fictional or real, to a dinner party, who would you include? Why?

MAPPING GUIDE

As noted earlier, there is no right or wrong way to create a role montage. I prefer to create mine on a large piece of paper. Others prefer to use a computer or the drawing program or app on their tablet device. Still others use cut-outs from magazines and newsprint to create their montage. No matter how you choose to design the art for your role montage, the process generally follows this outline:

- Begin with a blank sheet of paper and colored pens. Or if you want to use magazine cut-outs, get scissors and glue. If you are working on a computer, use different colored fonts.

- Put yourself in the center of the page.

- Write the names of people, characters, heroes, and others who have influenced or recognized your leadership. Put those who contributed the most or had the biggest impact closest to you in the center of the page, and those with less influence on the outside rim.

- List the qualities and attributes of the people and characters you chose under their names. These might include humor, self-confidence, strength, authenticity, perseverance or others. This will create a map or diagram of people and their distinctive elements that have influenced you and your leadership.

- Where possible, write a quote or metaphor that was supportive and inspiring to you for as many of the figures in your montage.

- Add a rating to each person by using numbers and a plus or minus sign. Use numbers from one to five. A five indicates that the influence has been greatest, and one is the least influential. Adding a plus sign indicates that the person or character has had an enduring influence on you over time. Using a negative sign indicates that the individual taught you what not to do.

- Use a color code.

  - The following color code is one that I use and you can use this one or create one of your own.

  - Use blue to circle names that indicate aspects of personality you aspire to or want to have.

  - Use green to circle the names of those who helped you to get where you are or where you want to be.

  - Use yellow to identify the aspects you already have and want to develop further.

  - Use orange for negative role models you want to avoid.

WHAT TO DO NEXT

Once you complete your role montage, review the influencers, mentors, role models, and other characters to see what you can glean about your leadership pathway. Notice the strengths that you have and also reflect on your development needs and challenges based on your montage. Once you have this information, you can decide what you want to address as you move forward and what will have the biggest impact on your career. You also will be able to assess new influencers in your life.

You can work on your montage with a friend, a group of friends, or with your team. You can also show your role montage to a coach or mentor to spur discussion and deeper exploration of goals and the key leadership qualities in your life.

The examples of role montage work that follow (see Figures 4.1 to 4.5) provide a variety of different ways to complete a role montage. The first role montage was completed by a consultant who was in her late forties and considering a career change. It is completed in Excel. The second example was completed at a leadership team building event by the team leader and facilitator. The third example, done with clip art, was completed by a mid-level manager at a large healthcare facility who wanted to improve her leadership abilities for a promotion. Two role montages done with magazine cut-outs and newsprint are also displayed at the end of this chapter.

CONCLUSION

The role montage process will help you identify influential figures that are a potent force in your life. It reinforces leadership attributes and self-awareness exploration as you seek to develop a plan for self-improvement. There is a step-by-step process for completing your own role montage, including questions for creating a list of influential people and characters, a color code, and questions to ask at the end of the process for a deeper understanding of self.

Chapter 4 Exercises

Getting Started

This exercise will guide you step by step through the process of designing your role montage. If you completed the exercises in the previous chapters, you will already have a list prepared for creating a role montage, while others might need to develop a list using this step-by-step guide. There is no right or wrong way to create a role montage.

You will find some examples of role montage work at the end of this chapter and examples of my own montages in Appendix C—Role Montage for the Ages.

Use the list that you developed earlier in this chapter or develop a list now of those who have impacted and inspired you. If there is someone you do not want to emulate, you can also include these people and note their negative qualities. If you have positive messages or stories include these influences also.

Designing Your Role Montage

Step 1

Make a list of influencers, their qualities, or any quotes that inspire you.

Who Has Influenced You?

_____

_____

List Their Qualities

_____

_____

What Quotes Inspired You?

_____

_____

Step 2

A good place to start your montage is with a large, blank piece of paper or a blank computer screen and a simple design program (standard in most computers). Put a representation of yourself at the center of the paper. Then place the other influencers from your list around yourself. Those closest to you in the center have had the most influence on you and fan out the others based on their impact on your leadership. Under each name include the qualities that you admire about them and the quotes that have impacted you.

Step 3

You can use a rating code (1–5) of who has had the most influence on you. If you rate a person +5, they have had a large impact. If the person has a rating of -4, they have given you negative traits that you do not want to follow. You can also use a color code described earlier in the chapter to distinguish the qualities that you want to emulate and develop more of and those that you think are already strengths.

Step 4

Once you have completed your role montage you can review it with friends, staff, or your team. An alternative is to reflect alone. Reflecting on the role montage you created will give you a sense of what you have accomplished so far in your leadership journey and in what areas you still need to grow.

Step 5

Ask yourself these questions.

- What leadership attributes do you admire in the people or characters you included in your montage?
- In what ways, do you see these attributes in your own leadership?
- What important messages did you learn from the stories behind the montage?
- How will you continue nurturing the development of these attributes?

CHAPTER 4

Role Montage

ROLE MONTAGE WORKSHEET

AGE	Teens	20s	30s	40s
GROUP				
High School	Mrs. Emerson +4 Clear Values and Ethics			
College		Prof. Smith +5 Strength and Wisdom		
Sports		Tennis Instructor +5 Competitive edge	Billie Jean King +3 Success as a Female Athlete	Tennis Partner +4 Competitive Player
Family	Brother +4 Humor	Sisters +4 Compassion	Spouse +5 Love, Fun	Two Children +5 Happiness
Church (choir, lector, altar girl) Music	Choir +5 Community	Bob Dylan +3 Transformation Protest/Change	Jazz +3 Spontaneity	Opera +5 Depth of Emotion
Work			Teaching +4 Love Subject Matter – Math	Consulting +5 Joy of Working

RATING: 1 = Low Influence 5 = High Influence
This role montage was completed by an IT consultant in her late forties.
A spreadsheet like this can be created in Microsoft Excel.

IT Consultant

FIGURE 4.1

FIGURE 4.2 Star Montage by Lily. Completed at retreat.

CHAPTER 4

Role Montage

This montage was created by a mid-level manager at a healthcare facility. She was being groomed for a higher-level job. As her coach, we worked on her leadership skills and used her role montage to inform her understanding of leadership and communication abilities.

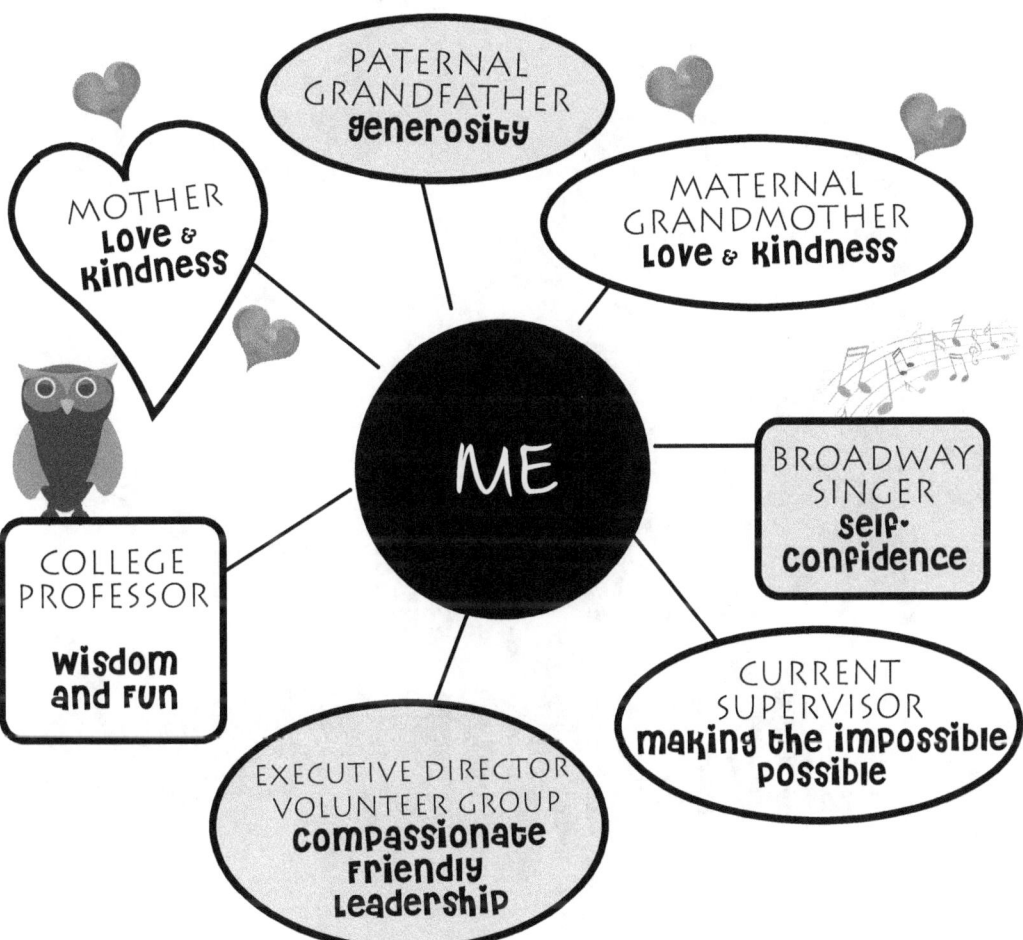

White boxes: Those who helped me get to where I want to be.
Gray Boxes: Aspects of personality that I aspire to or want to have.
Note: If this role montage was done in color using the color scheme from Chapter 4, the people in the gray boxes would actually be blue and the people in the white boxes would be green.
This montage uses clip art.

Mid-Level Manager — 2015

FIGURE 4.3

Role Montage

FIGURE 4.4

Role Montage

FIGURE 4.5

Chapter 5
PERSONAL APPLICATION OF ROLE MONTAGE

In This Chapter

- Two Principal Practices
- Meditation Practice
- Zazen Meditation
- Finding a Quiet Space
- Reflection Practice
- Self-Observation and Learning from Mistakes
- Reading, Observation, and Imitation
- Physical Practices
- Conclusion
- Chapter 5 Exercises

The methods and practices discussed in this chapter—especially the sections on meditation and reflection—are skills that effective leaders need to develop. Although it will take some effort to incorporate these inward-looking practices into your life, it's worth the effort; a realization even the over-scheduled leaders who participated in my study recognized.

The application options that follow are largely individually oriented and are geared toward incorporating the practices into life's familiar routines. Still, it's possible to take a group approach, for example, by bringing together friends to help examine and reflect on the role montage each of you has developed on your own using some of the practices suggested in this chapter.

> *Mindfulness is often spoken of as the heart of Buddhist meditation. It's not about Buddhism, but about paying attention. That's what all meditation is, no matter what tradition or particular technique is used.*
>
> —Jon Kabat-Zinn

TWO PRINCIPAL PRACTICES

People often confuse meditation and reflection.

The point of **meditation** is to gain control of your mind by ignoring all the whirling ideas and mental processes that normally occupy your consciousness. It is an ancient discipline that involves contemplation while focusing your mind on a thought, your breath, or an object. Using meditation techniques that concentrate on the breath will slow mental distractions and thought fragmentation to allow your mind to relax while thoughts, images, and other sensations fade into the background.[15]

Distractions and our tendencies to let our minds wander is a natural inclination, but if we gently bring ourselves back to focusing on our breath, it is possible to overcome this tendency and gain the solitude necessary to do role montage work. For those who are beginning to learn mindfulness, setting up one day per week to be mostly in silent practice and having a way to remind yourself at the moment you awake and doing all tasks with ease is how you stay in mindfulness. Do all movements slowly, evenly, and without reluctance.[16]

Meditation helps us pay attention to what's important in our lives (as Kabat-Zinn pointed out in the sidebar quote) and thus it's an effective tool for building and refining your role montage. While many choose to practice this mind-calming technique alone, I personally like group meditation, since it lets me tap into the energy of others who are meditating.

Reflection is a practice that is focused on taking action. You immerse yourself in a particular challenge or issue until you have worked out a way forward or made a decision about how to pursue an idea or face a challenge. Reflection is also a good tool for your role montage work, because it is a conscious evaluation of what influences the decisions we make.

MEDITATION PRACTICE

Some leaders I interviewed in my study considered meditation a useful practice because it helped them focus on the most important motivators in their lives. These leaders also said meditation has the additional benefit of helping them become more effective leaders and human beings. For example, Li Chen, a high-technology company leader, who was discussed in an earlier chapter, told me she found that meditating helped clarify her values and made her more courageous at her job. After Li Chen worked on a role montage, she used the montage to meditate on her leadership practices and how those she identified in her montage had influenced her the most.

Meditation practice exists in many forms. One type of meditation is called mindfulness meditation, a Zen technique that focuses on breath and the observation of emotions as they come and go. Mindfulness is considered the heart of Buddhist meditation, but its essence is universal and of deep practical benefit to all.

Mindfulness meditation has to do with waking up and living in harmony with oneself and the world. It has to do with examining who we are, with questioning our view in the world, and our place in it. Mindfulness means paying attention in a particular way: on purpose, in the present moment, and non-judgmentally. It is a natural activity that, like any other skill, requires developing. Mindfulness is like other skills that become effortless and automatic with practice.[17] If we are fully present when we complete a role montage, we will be able to realize the depth and richness of our possibilities for growth and transformation.[18]

ZAZEN MEDITATION

Zazen is the form of meditation at the heart of Zen practice. In fact, Zen is known as the "meditation school" of Buddhism. Basically, zazen is the study of the self. The great Master Dogen said, "To study the Buddha Way is to study the self, to study the self is to forget the self, and to forget the self is to be enlightened by the ten thousand things."[19] To be enlightened by the ten thousand things is to recognize the unity of the self and the ten thousand things. Upon his own enlightenment, Buddha was in seated meditation; Zen practice returns to the same seated meditation again and again.

For 2,500 years that meditation has continued, from generation to generation; it's the most important thing that has been passed on. It spread from India to China, to Japan, to other parts of Asia, and then finally to the West. It's a simple practice. It's easy to describe and easy to follow. But like all other practices, we have to engage it on a consistent basis if we want to discover its power and depth.

We tend to see body, breath, and mind separately, but in zazen they come together as one reality. The first thing to pay attention to is the position of the body in zazen. The body has a way of communicating outwardly to the world and inwardly to the self. How you position your body has a lot to do with what happens with your mind and your breath.

The most effective positioning of the body for the practice of zazen is the stable, symmetrical position of the seated Buddha. Sitting on the floor is recommended because it is grounded. We use a zafu—a small pillow—to raise the behind just a little, so that the knees can touch the ground. With your bottom on the pillow and two knees touching the ground, you form a tripod base that is natural, grounded, and stable.

Some of my participants used mindfulness meditation or a similar Buddhist practice, while others used a Christian meditation practice focused on prayer and working with the thoughts that surfaced as a result of prayers. The meditative path you take to these personal and career revelations is not important. It's more about the results.

Take Alma for example. Alma finds her meditation practice usually brings her peace and forgiveness through her focus on the Dalai Lama who is also part of her role montage. As the Dalai Lama points out, "It is the mind that exerts the greatest influence…we should devote our most serious efforts to bringing about mental peace…I have found that the greatest degree of inner tranquility comes from the development of love and compassion."[20]

FINDING A QUIET SPACE

One of the biggest obstacles to meditation is getting our minds to quiet down. The other obstacle is carving out time to focus on the practice. On that topic my own meditation teacher often told me, "If you can only meditate for five minutes every day then do it, or if only for one minute that will be enough to get started." This is a perspective I share with clients who want to meditate but don't believe they have the time to "do it right." In fact, the cure for this hesitation is simply to take that "one minute" path and build up the length of the session while your confidence in the practice increases.

One of my clients told me that his "racing mind" prevented him from taking advantage of meditation. In response I designed a special meditation that required him to count backward from one hundred by sevens. The mental processes involved in subtraction allowed the client to tame his thoughts enough so that he could use meditation techniques. Once he had learned to meditate, he could focus on his role montage and examine his leadership effectiveness.

The fact of the matter is that when your mind is still and you calm your true thoughts your authentic self is allowed to surface. Meditation is an extremely effective way to learn about your leadership behaviors and evaluate what you have and have not accomplished and, more important, what you want to accomplish in life.

REFLECTION PRACTICE

Reflection, as noted, is a more active way for leaders to contemplate a new or more effective path to follow. The leaders in my study told me that their own re-

> *Without reflection, we go blindly on our way, creating more unintended consequences, and failing to achieve anything useful.*
>
> —Margaret J. Wheatley

flective practices ranged from simply sitting quietly in their chairs, to taking long walks, to participating in strenuous exercise. However, walking was one of the most frequent responses given as a way to work through and solve difficult problems or challenges.

But no matter what approach the leaders said they took, the overwhelming benefit cited by the leaders was that better decisions were made as a result of such calm reflection (as the Margaret Wheatley sidebar quote suggests). My own experience also supports this conclusion. That's why I begin each day with a reflection practice focused on my day and its priorities. The practice keeps me centered on the most important tasks and grounds me deeply into my roots.

Practicing reflection as part of the montage process will help you hone in on past key influencers and will likely have the additional benefit of improved decision making. The exercise is also a useful tool to help leaders build self-awareness and increase effectiveness. As Heifetz and Linsky note in their 2002 *Harvard Business Review* article about key skills for leaders, strong reflection practices have a definite benefit:

> *You must establish a safe harbor where each day you can reflect on the previous day's journey, repair the psychological damage you have incurred, renew your stores of emotional resources, and recalibrate your moral compass.*

Your haven might be a physical place...or a regular routine, such as a daily walk through the neighborhood.[21]

Clearly, the benefits of reflection are worth the investment of your time. One leader I worked with told me that he used a key figure, Dr. Martin Luther King Jr., in his role montage to make some tough staffing decisions. As he walked to work, he would use the time to reflect on the montage that he had done at a recent retreat. It supported him in making the difficult decisions that he knew he had to make, like downsizing some of his staff. He said the regular reflective walks he took helped him access and apply Dr. King's legacy of not backing down from tough decisions to his own leadership situation and allowed his true leadership capabilities to surface.

Another participant in the study said she used her reflection time to compare her leadership montage aspirations with the new feedback she was getting from her team. She said that the self-awareness she had built during the montage-building process and the reflective practices she initiated had allowed her to recognize true progress toward her goal of becoming a courageous and honest leader.

SELF-OBSERVATION AND LEARNING FROM MISTAKES

Self-observation is a learned practice that all leaders need to develop. Some of the leaders in my study set up self-observation practices to deliberately note how others responded to their behaviors, gestures, and attitudes. They reported that this exercise greatly enhanced the role montage process and brought surprising insight. Ingrid, an attorney, who wanted to attain a partner position, told me about her self-assessment experience:

My most important learning comes from my mistakes. I spend time reflecting on what I did and how I have to change a situation so I don't make the same mistake twice. My first step is to recognize that I've made one, then to admit my mistake to others, and also say to myself that it's okay to make mistakes.

I feel vulnerable and that is a difficult emotion in my firm but I have to accept it's alright to feel that way. I never believe that I know it all. I believe learning through failure is the best way to learn.

Fran, a healthcare executive, told me she had "a fear of failure, so I need to put more belief on my gut as I gather information…from the people I respect. I believe that mistakes are learning opportunities." She said self-observation exercises helped her learn from her mistakes and listen to her heart, her mind, and her intuition in situations where she made mistakes.

Learning from mistakes is how many self-aware people grow their emotional intelligence. They pay attention to the feedback they are receiving, and they spend time reflecting on what will move them toward improving or correcting their behaviors or actions. In Appendix A, the Values and Feedback Exercise will help you better understand your reaction to feedback after you complete the exercise and answer the questions provided.

READING, OBSERVATION, AND IMITATION

Of course, there are other ways you can learn about yourself. Reading, observing, and imitating the behaviors of others are far less costly ways to build self-awareness than coaching and counseling; and, most important, the source material on building leadership capabilities is nearly inexhaustible.

Judith, a president of a large national organization, said that she used books as a main source for her own learning. She also said she was a keen observer and even imitator of other people with skills and behaviors she admired. For specific help, Judith said she hired a coach to help her:

I like to learn. I like to pick up new information and be always growing and looking for opportunities to learn about myself…books on a specific topic that I am trying to learn about {help} me understand how I can be a better person and more effective leader. I read a lot of self-help books on awareness and leadership.

I read every nonfiction book about a topic, for example, when we're engaging in teambuilding, I read everything there was. On my bedside table now, there are lots of books on strategic planning.

Leaders like Judith offer a good example of the range of montage development options. If you are able to read books and make observations to figure out the next steps for your own career or organization's future that's a perfectly good path. Remember, it's about the destination, not so much how you get there.

PHYSICAL PRACTICES

Some participants in the study said they used physical practices, such as exercise or yoga practice, during their time of reflection and introspection. If going to the gym four or five times each week or taking a dance or yoga class (or any kind of physical activity for that matter) helps you build an effective role montage, it's a perfectly acceptable pathway. After all, the goal is to understand who you are and part of that journey is confidently picking the best path for you and the kind of leader you want to be.

CONCLUSION

Personal applications of role montage exploration aid in the exploration of your deepest values and enhance self-awareness. You can use any of the activities noted in this chapter for this purpose: meditation, reflection, self-observation, learning from mistakes, reading, imitation, and physical practices. Examining your role montage pictures in concert with these activities provides valuable insight into your baseline values and how they connect with the type of leader you want to become. Essential messages about our leadership strengths and challenges will reveal themselves, such as fairness, perfectionism, and micromanaging, when we focus on our role montages and use them as personal tools.

The interviewed leaders used many of the methods discussed in this chapter on their journey to self-understanding and leadership effectiveness. This capacity for self-examination was voiced by one leader who told me the answer was simply to "be a lifelong learner." It's advice I'm sure all the leaders I interviewed would absolutely endorse.

Chapter 5 Exercises

Getting Started

This exercise along with those offered in previous chapters helps you identify personal practices to enhance your role montage experience. Meditation and reflection are the most impactful ones since they can be taught and practiced. There are meditation centers in many locations and they teach various kinds of meditation and reflection practices. It is important for leaders to spend time learning meditation and reflection or enhancing what's already known. These valuable tools combined with role montage can assist in increasing self-understanding.

Exercise A

Consider the full landscape of the personal practices that you've done in your life. It's essential to review the practices cited in this chapter and consider which ones you have tried and which ones you do on a regular basis. What's most important is that you begin the process of identifying these practices in your life and committing something to paper or electronic documenting on the associated website.

List the practices that you do for developing your self-awareness (meditation, reflection, self-observation, learning from mistakes, reading, imitation, and physical practices). Take time to consider how these practices have impacted your journey toward becoming an effective leader. Examine your self-awareness and consider whether or not you need to develop more practices. You can jot down the answers either in this book or use the online forms available www.rolemontage.com.

_____

_____

_____

_____

_____

_____

_____

Enhancing Personal Application Practices with Role Montage

What are my personal practices?

_____

_____

What practices are enhanced by using my role montage? Explain.

_____

_____

What practices do I want to increase, enhance, or add?

Make a commitment to do that practice.

_____

_____

Chapter 6
APPLYING WHAT YOU LEARNED IN THE WORKPLACE

In This Chapter

- Team Building

- Workshops and Training

- Coaching and Consulting

- Feedback

- Conclusion

- Chapter 6 Exercises

Role montage practice can have practical applications beyond personal development. You can apply what you've learned in this book at a workplace team-building retreat, a workshop, a training session, or during a coaching or a feedback session. Manager and individual contributors can use the self-reflection tools regardless of their intention to apply their work to a role montage.

> *The future belongs to those who believe in the beauty of their dreams.*
>
> —Eleanor Roosevelt

This chapter discusses an application of role montage exploration for anyone willing to imagine a new future and to "believe in the beauty of their dreams," as Eleanor Roosevelt said in the sidebar quote.

TEAM BUILDING

Lily, a manager at a high-tech company, took her team offsite to build leadership skills and more synergy among the team members. She decided to use the role montage process at the retreat because her engineers were creative and independent but not always the most cohesive in their interactions. Lily asked each of the participants to design a role montage picture and share it. Lily's team members learned a great deal from the pictures they created and shared but it was only when they answered deeper reflection questions that the group grew closer as a team.

Here are the questions she asked:

- What leadership attributes do you admire in the people or characters you included in your montage?

- In what ways, do you see these attributes in your own leadership?

- What important messages did you learn from the stories behind the montages?

- How will you continue nurturing the development of these attributes and how can the team help you with that work?

Lily told me that the team-building exercise was a success. After the retreat, the engineers communicated in a different way with one another, and it was clear that they had bonded and built positive, long-term leadership behaviors.

Role montage practice can be taught to teams and groups as the example above illustrates. While taking your team off-site is a desirable option, it can be just as effective to hold a team-building workshop in an office conference room or any other available quiet space at your work site. As long as your group can take advantage of the creative and artistic nature of the experience, the physical surroundings are not that critical since the process is fairly straightforward.

The first task in such a role montage retreat is for individual team members to build their own role montage. This process will require some amount of facilitated training. Still, once these individual role montages are created, team members can gather and share their role montage drawings with one another. They can share their choices of the people or characters that populate their montages and why the messages embodied in their choices are important to them.

Sharing these important influences is a meaningful experience that brings the team together at a deeper, more personal level. The benefits of this exercise clearly increase communication and allow authentic leadership to grow. The team leader or a manager can facilitate this process, but using an internal or external consultant to facilitate the exercise makes the exercise more effective for all participants, including the leader or manager.

WORKSHOPS AND TRAINING

Role montage exploration can also be used by organizations to help their managers and other leaders build leadership behaviors and increase self-awareness as an alternative to attending external personal growth or leadership training workshops. For example, a former corporate human resources executive, Gwen, told me that she had successfully used role montage exploration as a way to learn more about herself and her leadership capabilities. Gwen said her role montage experience allowed her to examine her leadership strengths and challenges and helped her make positive changes that made her a better, more empathetic leader.

I love learning and opportunities for growth. I took lots of experiential learning classes, training workshops, and even had coach training. I constructed a role montage in one workshop. After these experiences, I saw leadership possibilities and changed my management style. I'm not such a perfectionist, and I don't expect my team to be, either. I realized that I only could be effective in helping others after I knew who I was.

The role montage experience permits leaders to examine themselves in a specific setting and then apply what they've learned to their work. Another example is Ming, a former executive in a global company. She said that the "real time" feedback she got through the experience was more powerful than either her 360-degree feedback experience or any other high-potential training that she had received during her corporate career. Ming's experience is not unusual, especially for leaders who enjoy learning and drawing supportive conclusions with others. It is not as effective, however, for the leaders who prefer more one-on-one interaction for processing self-discovery.

COACHING AND CONSULTING

Coaching and consulting are two effective tools that leaders can use for gaining self-awareness and building their leadership capabilities in a profound way. Emma explained to me how her team and its consulting experiences helped build her self-awareness and allowed her to better understand her leadership role when she worked in the nonprofit arena.

As a leader, self-awareness helped me realize that I had to do certain things for the organization to move forward. I hired a consultant to help me. In the past, I often did everything myself, but I had to rely on my team more and more. They taught me the most about leadership and how to be a good leader. My consultant helped me take difficult steps with the Board. She showed me that the Board needed to be reconfigured and reorganized in order to move the organization ahead. I was unable to make these changes myself, because I didn't want to hurt any of the long-time board members. I was fortunate to have a consultant who recognized what we needed to do and helped me do it.

The benefits of working with consultants are many and include gaining objective viewpoints, clarification of issues, and insight into how other organizations have faced similar issues. Consultants can use the role montage experiences to help individuals in the organization see change management issues from a different perspective.

Coaching, on the other hand, involves identification of a person's style and strengths in addition to areas for development. The coach helps the client discover his or her strengths and challenges by using a variety of assessment tools. Once the assessment is finished, a development plan guides the client to become a more effective, self-confident leader.

Chloe, a leader in the financial industry, told me she had an executive coach who was a "sounding board" for her. She had a stressful job because the organization was undergoing a great deal of upheaval.

I was fortunate to have an external executive coach; my company wanted to invest in me. Coaching was viewed as a perk in our company. We also received a three-day internal coaching and leadership workshop for senior executives, a breakfast speakers' series, and a book list of titles to read so that all executives read the same books.

For emerging leaders, it is important to negotiate for coaching and other "perks" as part of their acceptance package for new leadership positions. There are less costly options discussed in this chapter, such as training programs and workshops that are an alternative to one-on-one coaching.

Here's how another participant described her coaching experience:

I didn't have the privilege of coaching until I went to a larger company that offered it. I think coaching is effective because I know when I'm being coached the intention is to help me. Sometimes people give feedback, and there are filters in it making the information difficult to trust. For example, I worry about the politics involved in receiving feedback from certain people. I don't have this concern when my coach gives me feedback, because, we deal with issues right then in the room, we go straight to the

> *heart of the matter, and I believe that I get a more objective view from my coach.*

In times of economic downturn, organizations might not be so ready to provide many of these "perks." When this occurs many leaders consider it a good investment to seek out and pay for coaches or consultants on their own.

Both consultants and coaches can use the role montage process with their clients. See Appendix F for instructions. The questions used in the role montage process are engaging and help individual clients be more collaborative and authentic and encourage the building of stronger, more cohesive teams.

FEEDBACK

Feedback gives leaders more knowledge about their behaviors and the developmental challenges they face. Feedback is defined as information about past behavior delivered in the present that might influence future behavior.[22] It's a process of giving, receiving, and analyzing advice or observation and can lead to greater self-awareness. In order to change behavior, individuals have to take in feedback and utilize it for altering their actions. Role montage can facilitate sharing of this valuable feedback through individual or coached work. Managers can also work directly with employees to build and use the personal and professional information found using the role montage process.

There are two types of feedback; one is informal and the other is formal. The informal kind usually requires people to solicit feedback on their own. Some leaders solicit feedback by asking directly how they are perceived by their teams and the people around them. (See Appendix D for feedback forms.) They ask the right questions and then listen non-defensively to show that they are open to both positive and negative feedback. This approach demonstrates how making the leader vulnerable in the feedback process can lead to self-awareness and a willingness to learn.[23]

Most organizations use a formal process, such as the multi-rater feedback approach known as 360-degree feedback. The process asks people from different vantage points (employer, peers, and direct reports) to rate the leader, manager, or supervisor or team member on a set of managerial skills and abilities.[24] The data is collected and synthesized by a coach or consultant. The goal is to help people understand how they are perceived by their various constituents and to gain self-awareness about their actions and behaviors. When it is used for gaining self-awareness, the focus is on development and not on assessment of performance. It is usually a confidential process facilitated by an expert, neutral, third party.

Samantha, a healthcare leader who was helping her organization make a major shift using a large change management process, said that the feedback she received helped her be a more self-aware leader. "I've been told that I'm too bossy, and it can get in my way when I'm leading, because some people are turned off.

I have to get them onboard when they are essential to the project." Sam used both informal and formal feedback processes to help her learn about her challenges and her strengths.

I actually think it's been very critical for me to get feedback to make me a better leader, because people's perceptions are their reality. I've always been open to feedback, and I seek it out if there's no formal 360-degree process at work. Informal or formal feedback has been useful to me. I like to understand people's perceptions of me and where I can improve.

Sam's responsiveness to feedback assisted her self-learning and enabled her to develop her leadership.

Teams also offer feedback, as discussed earlier in the chapter. When completing a role montage, the feedback and questions we get as a result of an offsite group or team feedback is an essential part of the learning. We observe ourselves and then imitate the people and characters in our montage.

The leaders I interviewed told me that their teams held them accountable for their behaviors and they listened to the feedback to improve their leadership. These were leaders who wanted to know how people perceived them and so solicited feedback that they were open to receiving when it was offered. They were curious about how others saw them and they wanted the feedback in order to change their behaviors and be more productive leaders.

I consulted to a high-tech company where a formal 360-degree process was used for all top leaders. Marco, a director who was required to get feedback, told me:

The first time I had 360-degree feedback, I was sorry that I didn't do it sooner, because it was one of the most worthwhile things that I've ever completed. It helped me understand myself more and enabled me to be a better leader.

Marco used his 360-degree feedback to change his behavior and become more influential and less confrontational. He also designed a role montage as part of our coaching process. By listing the important people in his life he discovered that their messages contained some of the same feedback he received in the 360-degree process. It helped him understand his leadership style and how others experienced his behavior.

In addition to role montage and formal organizational 360-degree feedback programs, consultants have many other feedback options to use, including a number of well-regarded assessment tools. Some of the ones I typically use are MBTI (Myers-Briggs Type Indicator),[25] LSI (Kolb Learning Style Inventory),[26] and TKI (Thomas-Kilmann Conflict Mode Instrument).[27]

For some leaders these more formalized methods for gaining self-awareness and getting or receiving feedback are more comfortable than a practice such as meditation or self-reflection.

CONCLUSION

All the practices discussed in this chapter are used in workplaces to ensure the advancement of leaders and especially those with high potential. The most effective leaders exhibit curiosity and an insatiable hunger for knowledge and learning. They do not want to become stagnant and instead challenge themselves to be more self-aware and more empathetic to the people around them in both work and personal situations. They view the work of self-development as a lifelong process and are open to using a variety of pathways, including coaching, role montage, feedback, workshops, and assessments.

I found that leaders who took the time and effort got real results and forged stronger relationships with their teams and the other people in their organizations and had the self-awareness and confidence to view themselves as successful leaders.

Chapter 6 Exercises

TOOLKIT FOR LEARNING ABOUT SELF

What follows is a simple toolkit that will help jumpstart your self-awareness journey. As with the other exercises and tools offered in this book, you can find an electronic version by logging on to www.rolemontage.com.

Getting Started

When faced with a challenge or obstacle or the need to learn something new, do you tend to turn **inward** or seek learning by looking **outward** and engaging others? Choose one: Inward or Outward

If you chose Inward, then the practices that would be most effective for you are:

1. Reflection/Prayer
2. Meditation
3. Reading
4. Observation
5. Imitation

Of the five listed above, rank them by putting the one you practice the most or would practice the most first. Which one(s) do you practice now? Which one(s) would you like to try out?

If you chose Outward, then the practices that would be most effective for you are:

1. Coaching

2. Consulting

3. Counseling or Therapy

4. Personal Growth Workshops

5. Training

Of the five listed above, rank them by putting the one you practice the most or would practice the most first. Which one(s) do you practice now? Which one(s) would you like to try out?

If you are more of an inward learner, you can still try any of the five practices listed for outward learner. Sometimes an internally focused person can benefit from coaching by using a coach who helps him or her focus internally in a new way. Likewise, the externally-focused person might gain some new insights by practicing a reflection technique.

Take this opportunity to choose one of the opposite practices to engage in.

Write down how that experience affected you and incorporate journaling into your practices.

_____

_____

Please answer the following questions:

- What is your plan to accomplish one of these practices in the next month?

  _____

- When will you practice?

  _____

- What time of day?

  _____

- For how much time?

  _____

Feedback is important to both inward- and outward-looking learners.

- How do you accept feedback?

_____

- How can you learn more about your reactions to receiving difficult feedback?

_____

- What is your plan to seek feedback from your team? From your manager?

_____

There are many online tools and books that can help you complete an assessment and decide your personality type. One free tool is the Personal Style Inventory (PSI) by R. Craig Hogan and David W. Champagne.[28] It is a tool for individuals or teams and provides results that are similar to understanding your Myers-Briggs type. Another tool is the Enneagram[29] that has a more spiritual component than the Myers-Briggs and can be useful in work settings. There are many other assessments and tools that are available to help you understand yourself and your team more completely.

Appendices

ABOUT THE APPENDICES

The appendices contain supplemental information and material that will support you in your role montage creation experience. As noted throughout this book, you can either respond directly to the questions or exercises in the book or go to the associated website, www.rolemontage.com, and download a separate copy.

Here's what's included in the appendices:

- Appendix A—Values Exercise and Feedback Exercise

- Appendix B—Role Montage Worksheet Example

- Appendix C—Role Montage for the Ages

- Appendix D—Forms for Getting Feedback

- Appendix E—Prototypes of Role Montage Pictures

- Appendix F—For Coaches and Consultants: How to Use Role Montage Practice

APPENDIX A—VALUES EXERCISE

Exercise 1

This exercise, as noted in Chapter 1, is designed to help you determine what areas in your life need more attention. It suggests a way to prioritize them for the future. The exercise encourages you to identify your own values. This is an important first step toward greater self-awareness. As noted throughout this book, self-awareness is a key to decision-making capability and will help you understand problems, such as poor motivation and procrastination, that might be hindering your movement forward.

Values are the beliefs that we hold dearly. In a values-clarification exercise you are prompted to better understand yourself and how you define your own values. You will be asked to reflect on a list of possible values (and add any you think are important). Then you'll rate the values **H** for high, **M** for medium, and **L** for low. Once you've done this work, then you pick the top five and explain their importance in your life and work.

A second pass at your values list asks you to narrow your list to only three values. With this list of three in mind, you're prompted to close your eyes and envision a world that only has one value for you to live by. The ultimate test of your chosen value is to complete the values exercise while imagining a situation where it is not possible to honor that value. The degree of "craziness" of that choice will reveal how important that value is to you.

Values List

__ Achievement	__ Freedom	__ Responsibility
__ Caring	__ Fun	__ Risk
__ Caution	__ Growth	__ Security
__ Challenge	__ Harmony	__ Service to others
__ Communication	__ Honesty & integrity	__ Speed
__ Competition	__ Beauty	__ Humor
__ Cooperation	__ Individualism	__ Recognition
__ Collaboration	__ Innovation	__ Uniqueness
__ Creativity	__ Involvement	__ Winning
__ Curiosity	__ Learning	__ Wisdom
__ Compassion	__ Wealth	__ Spirituality
__ Determination	__ Productivity	__ Health
__ Diversity	__ Love	__ Exercise
__ Fairness	__ Quality	__ Variety
__ Family time	__ Respect	
__ Flexibility	__ Success	

—Source: *The Coaches Training Institute Course Manual*

Exercise 2
Values and Feedback Exercise

The following exercise can be done individually or with a group of friends or colleagues. This exercise allows you to understand your values and how you are affected by feedback.

1. Write down all the words that you use to describe yourself or that others have told you describe you. These might include some of your important values as contained in the matrix of values in the Values List in Exercise 1.

2. If you're doing the exercise individually, then skip to the questions below. If this is a group exercise, then continue.

3. Put up a flip chart with the words you have chosen to describe yourself, or you can hand out to all the participants the words on a sheet of paper. Allow blank space for participants to write their descriptions and ask them to cross out those words that are not a fit for how they see you.

4. Tell the group you are interested in receiving more feedback and also in understanding your relationship to feedback.

5. Ask the group to place their words on sticky notes (one word per note) and place the note on a flip chart, where you have written all the words you used to describe yourself.

6. Ask for feedback from the group about the words they chose to describe you. See if they align with your values. Notice your reaction to the feedback. Discuss with the group your feelings and emotions toward feedback.

7. Once you've gone through the exercise answer the questions provided below:

What did you learn from this experience?

_____

_____

What did you learn from your reaction to feedback from the group?

_____

_____

What can you do to be more self-observant and honest in your assessment of yourself?

_____

_____

You can jot down the answers either in this book or use the online form available www.rolemontage.com.

APPENDIX B—
ROLE MONTAGE WORKSHEET EXAMPLE

The following sample Role Montage Worksheet was completed by a vice president of human resources at a large hospital. She was known to watch "the backs" of her staff and they in turn watched hers. Their previous supervisor did not do this. He took credit for what they did and didn't protect them. When the new VP first came to the hospital, it took her awhile to gain the trust of her staff. This example shows how she completed this worksheet.

Instructions

Exercise A

Make a list of those who have influenced you the most.

_____

_____

Exercise B

Consider the list you made in Exercise A of people who have influenced you. Take some time to consider these people and the impact they have had on your journey toward becoming an effective leader. As you consider the traits that you admire, make a notation if you share these qualities or if there is a deficit that you want to fill. This will help you form a development plan for the future. It will show the areas you need to find additional mentors, role models, coaches, and other resources.

Who has influenced you?	What qualities do you admire about these people? What qualities do you want to emulate?	What are the negative qualities these people might have? What qualities do you not want to emulate?
My dad	Caring, loving, humor, good leadership qualities	
Teacher in 5th grade	Safety patrol, leadership work	
Best friend	Loyalty, health, trust	
Staff person	Recognition	Unhealthy food choices
Florence Nightingale	Caring and well-being	Stubbornness

What qualities do you share with your role montage choices?	How can you develop the qualities that you don't share with your role montage choices	How will these qualities move you toward your leadership goals?
Caring		Recognizing staff and good work they do builds trust important to leadership
Humor	I could enhance my quality of humor by listening to comedians and reading humorous books.	Sense of humor—good for effective leaders
Health	I could take better care of my health by eating healthy foods and exercising regularly (4x/week)	Health is vital to leadership

APPENDIX C—ROLE MONTAGE FOR THE AGES

When completing a role montage, I reflect on whether my current mentors, role models, and characters are different from the ones I've chosen at other times in my life. For example, when I first drew my role montage in the 1980s, my picture was a daisy with me in the center. The petals of the flower were the influencers from that time in my life. As I finished graduate school, many of my influencers were the deans, faculty, and advisors from the experiences I had while a graduate student.

The montage below was completed after I finished my doctorate in the early 1980s. I was giving workshops for women on balancing their personal and professional lives. I was curious about how the women I met depicted themselves on their montage and how those around them helped to balance their lives. My interest was in role harmony.

Personally, I usually reflect on whether some of my influencers, mentors, and role models are more enduring than others. I was surprised to discover as a result of writing this book how my own choices had evolved throughout the years and how much the picture that I drew changed.

I realized that I wanted to show in the new role montage the overlapping influences and the fact that some people had more influence than others. Those closest to me in the center hold greater influence. I also drew some who were not as close to me, and I placed them farther out on the circle. There is a change in the influencers from the 1980s to my current role montage.

Role Montage

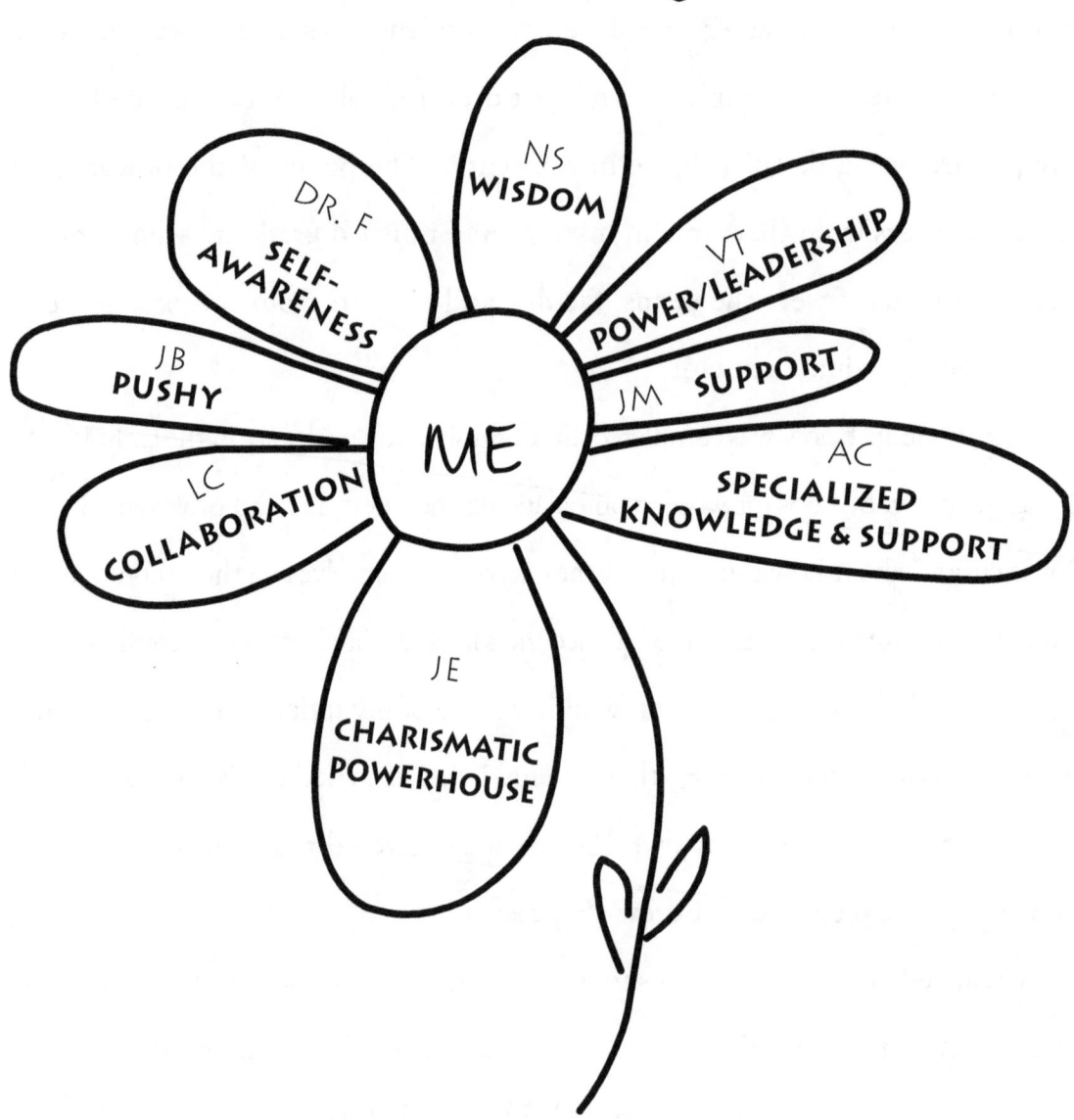

Jan M. Schmuckler, PhD – 1980s

APPENDIX C 121

Role Montage

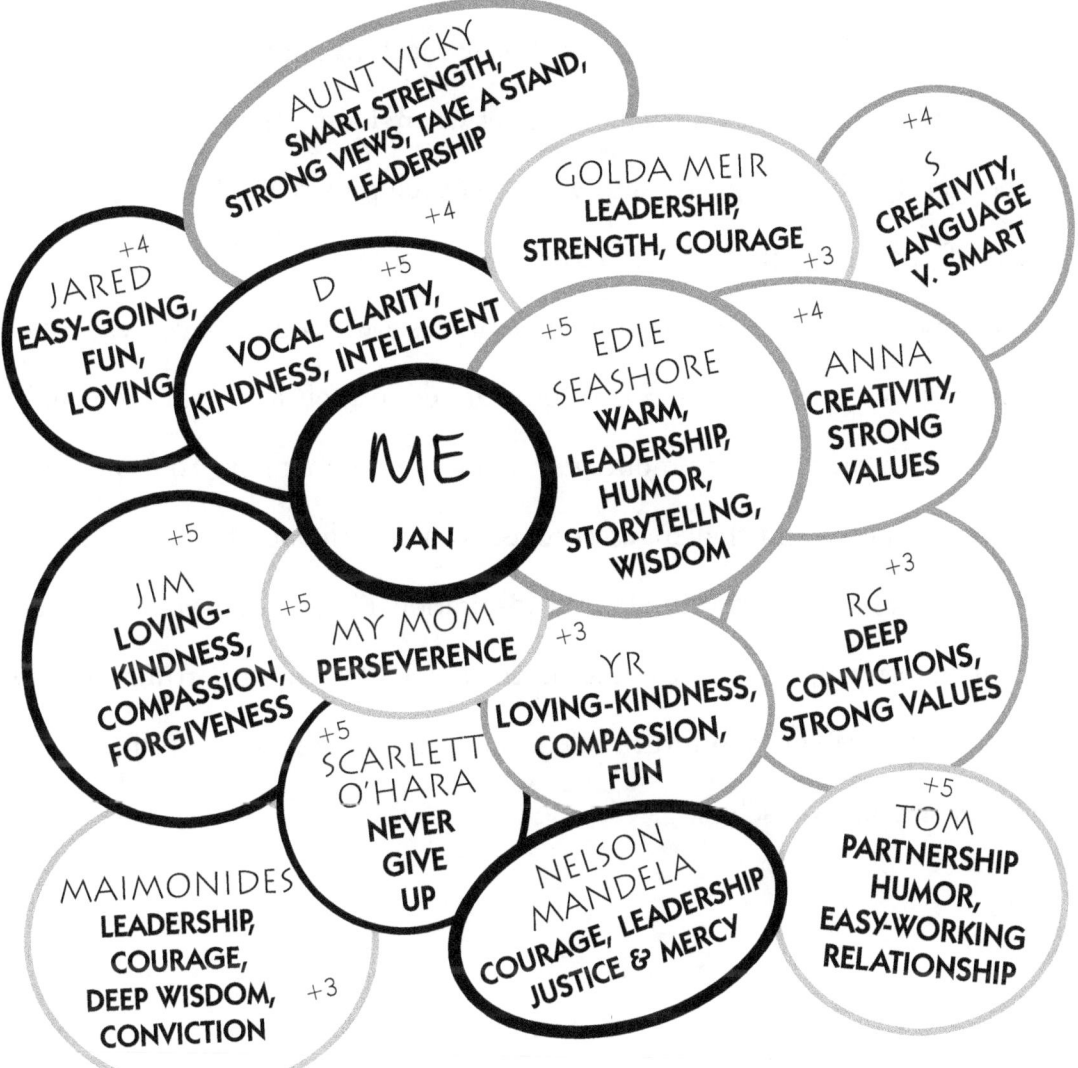

Heavy black lines indicate aspects of personality that I aspire to or want to have.

Jan M. Schmuckler, PhD – 2015

APPENDIX 1.2

I create my montages with a large piece of paper and many colored pens. Beneath the names is an explanation or quality of what I admired in that person. Actual names aren't used in this picture except for some of the people that I've mentioned in chapters of the book. The colors used have meaning; orange is a negative influence, green is someone who helped me get where I am, yellow is for the aspects of a person that I already have and want to develop further, and blue indicates aspects of personality that I aspire to or want to obtain.

I tell my clients to recreate their role montages every couple of years and compare results to see what has and has not changed in their leadership role and in their life. This review of the montage provides an opportunity to evaluate our development needs and challenges or to assess new influencers in our lives.

As we look back, we can visualize the inspirational forces we have encountered. As we look forward, we can see our aspirations. We have the opportunity to compare our past, present, and future role montages. This gives us a full picture of our leadership and ourselves.

APPENDIX D—FORMS FOR GETTING FEEDBACK

It can be difficult to ask for feedback. The following forms will make it easier to request feedback from professional and personal sources. Form 1 is the most basic about choosing the people you want to give you feedback.

Form 2 is a request for feedback by email that you can tailor to your needs to ask various people to participate in your feedback process. It can be an online survey or an interview by phone or in person.

Form 3 is a simplified version of questions to ask in getting feedback. The process of getting the feedback is often delegated to an internal consultant, a coach, or an external consultant. It is important to emphasize the confidential nature of the feedback.

The purpose in acquiring this feedback is to look for themes and patterns in the data collected, not for who said what. After the data has been collected, a plan is developed to address the challenges that you are facing in your leadership and what strengths you want to reinforce. It is important to reconnect with the people who gave you feedback and let them know what you expect to do about the results and what your plan is.

Form 1—How to Choose Your Feedback Raters

- Make a list of the people you want to ask to give you feedback.

- Choose those who will provide an accurate assessment of your behavior and skills.

- If you are asking friends, get a balanced point of view. In other words, don't just ask people who only see your positive contributions.

- If you are asking work colleagues, pick your manager, peers, and staff who report to you. You can also include customers or clients.

- The best timeframe in terms of people knowing you and being able to give accurate feedback is:

  - Up to six months is a first impression ONLY.

  - One year to less than five years is the ideal time for obtaining accurate feedback for development and/or performance.

- Review the people on your list with your manager.

Your Name _____

Rater Name   Relationship to You/Email

_____   _____

_____   _____

_____   _____

_____   _____

Follow-Up Interviews with People Who Have Agreed

Name   Telephone Number

_____   _____

_____   _____

_____   _____

_____   _____

—Adapted from 1998 audiotape of Robert (Bob) W. Eichinger

Form 2—Request for Feedback Form

Here is an example of how you might ask for participation. In the email, use words and idioms that are your own. If an online survey will be sent, inform the participant when the email and link to the survey might arrive. Include the name of the company that will be sending the email. If you are using a consultant or coach to collect the data, let the individual know the name and background of the person in order to recognize who is assisting you.

> Dear Person's Name:
>
> I would appreciate your participation in a feedback process I am initiating to give me more information for my professional and personal learning.
>
> I am gathering feedback about me to help determine an action plan to address any concerns and also help me grow as a leader. I need your input to help me make the necessary behavioral shifts to become more effective.
>
> Your interview will be set at your convenience by XXXX. The length of the interview is 30 minutes and will be confidential and anonymous. I am looking for general themes and patterns about my leadership in the multiple responses I receive, not for individuals and what might be specifically said.
>
> Please make yourself available when XXXX calls to set up your appointment. Or if you prefer to arrange this yourself, the calendaring is set up on Sign-up Genius {or another online calendaring service}.
>
> Thank you again for your continued support and commitment.
>
> Regards,
> Name
> Job Position

Form 3—Possible Questionnaire

First, explain the purpose of the feedback collection.

Second, tell the participant your background.

Third, ensure the participant about the confidentiality of the process. Tell them that only themes and patterns will be analyzed and given to the person requesting the feedback. After the process is complete, the participants will have a discussion with the leader to review the development plan, so they can see how their feedback was important to the overall process.

Fourth, begin by asking the person how long he or she has known the person who wants feedback and in what capacity they have known him or her.

Question #1: What are the strengths of _____?

Question #2: What are the areas for improvement?

Question #3: If you could offer one piece of advice for this person, what would it be?

Question #4: Is there anything that I haven't asked you that you think I need to know?

APPENDIX E— PROTOTYPES OF ROLE MONTAGE PICTURES

The prototypes displayed in this appendix are typical examples that clients and interviewed participants used in representing their role montages. They are created for your use if you would rather use a preformed example. The following pages have cognitive representations that you can use for designing your role montage. For anyone who feels that they are not artistic enough to develop one of their own, these prototypes can be useful.

The journey for creating a role montage is important and will help you identify strengths and areas of development. If you completed the exercises at the end of each chapter in this book, you will proceed on this pathway a little more quickly. No matter where you begin, you will derive inspiration and fulfillment from this process.

Getting Started

1. Choose a montage in this appendix that reflects you and your spirit.

2. Write down all the influencers you have or use those from the exercises at the end of each chapter.

3. Compile a list of quotes or punch lines from stories that these inspirational people gave you.

4. Decide if you are going to complete this montage by yourself or with friends.

5. Be sure to use colored pens or pencils. If using a computer-drawn image, use different fonts and colors. Use the color code in Chapter 4 or create your own.

6. If using magazines and newsprint, take a piece of stiff cardboard to glue the cut-outs onto. Choose a color of cardboard that you like and is big enough to display all your cut-outs. You might want to cut out the pictures before you decide on the size of cardboard that you will need. Snip words and headlines that convey the quotes and punch lines from stories. Arrange the pictures and headlines on the cardboard the way that most represents you.

7. Have fun!!

Choose one of the role montage images that appeals to you and get started!

Role Montage

Role Montage

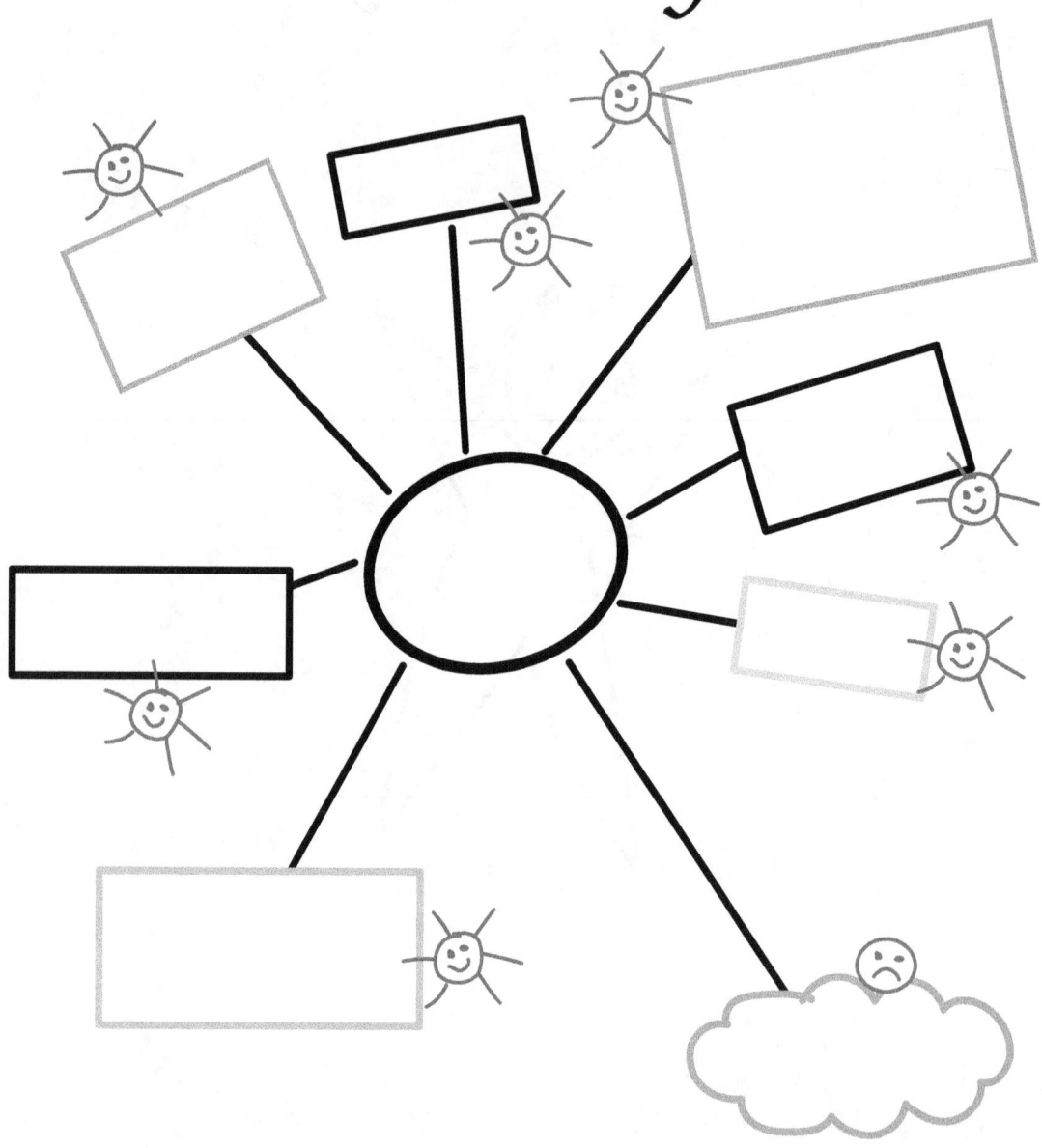

APPENDIX E

Role Montage

APPENDIX F—
FOR COACHES AND CONSULTANTS: HOW TO USE ROLE MONTAGE PRACTICE

The process of uncovering the internal motivational and inspirational drivers through role montage practice can be a benefit to your coaching and consulting clients. You can lead them through the process and ask them the questions offered in this appendix—see #5 and use questions a through e—to take them to a deeper self-realization level.

You can also help them discover missing leadership attributes and how to obtain the missing information or competencies through participation in training workshops or conferences or through reading or other self-instruction.

Getting Started

1. Tell your client to make a list of the important influences in their life or ask them to answer the questions in Chapter 4.

2. Give them a blank piece of paper to draw their montage.

3. Give them colored pens and pencils and discuss a color code with them (see Chapter 4). Or provide cardboard and magazines to do cut-outs and headlines to represent the important people and characters in their life.

4. Ask them to include the key phrases or quotes that these people offered them.

5. Once they have completed the montage, ask them the following questions.

   a. In what ways do you see these attributes in your own leadership?

   b. What important messages did you learn from the stories behind the montage?

   c. How will you continue nurturing the development of these attributes?

   d. What leadership attributes did you admire in the people or characters you included in your montage?

   e. If you are working with a team you can ask them, "How can the team help you with that work?"

6. Based on the answers to these questions, you can coach them to be more self-aware and successful.

Acknowledgments

I'm extremely grateful to the many people who recommended the leaders I interviewed for this book. I am indebted to these participants who gave their time and expertise so I could gain clarity and insights about role montage, leadership, and self-awareness. Many of my clients also contributed to the stories and ideas and I am deeply appreciative of them.

Mark Morrow, my editor and book coach, contributed greatly to this book in two ways. First, he recognized the value of the concept of the role montage process and suggested that I make it the focus of my book. Second, he gave me confidence in my writing while coaching and supporting me. I have enormous gratitude for Joni Wilson, my copyeditor and proofreader, who polished the manuscript and helped me on every final step. Deborah Perdue of Illumination Graphics, my illustrator extraordinaire, took the primitive drawings I gave her and created incredible illustrations to enliven the book. She took her time to work with me to get the illustrations of the montages, the cover, and the interior design just right. The back cover photograph was taken by Nate Fowle, Oakocalyptic Designs; I'm grateful to Nate for the ease of the photo shoot and the excellent photograph.

My writing group, Bev Scott and B. Kim Barnes, read endless copies of the chapters and answered my many questions about writing and the publishing process. They provided support above and beyond the call of duty.

Many friends and colleagues generously read early drafts and offered their thoughts. Deep thanks to Diane Bernbaum, Alice Collier Cochran, Anna Martin, Rose Singer, and others too numerous to mention individually. I am most appreciative to those in my focus groups who helped me realize who my "true" audience for the book is.

I am fortunate to have many loving friends and family who have offered me unconditional support during the years I've been writing this book, such as my sisters, Joy and Aviva, Emily Jarosz, Maurice Monette, and many others. My women's group served as thought partners and indulged me by completing their own montages on several occasions. I'm grateful to my friends, whether your name is mentioned here or not.

I'm indebted to many critical readers of the second manuscript, which focused on role montage, especially Sally Hunter, Tom Ucko, Mieko Diener and Alex Witte (my Millennial team), and Rita Sever, who used role montage for her leadership retreat.

Finally, I am deeply thankful for my great good fortune to have the support, love, and encouragement of my husband, Jim Martin, who has been patient during this process and offered wise advice when needed. I am grateful for my children, Anna and Jared, and their friends who sat at my dinner table and discussed the ideas in this book with me. I especially hope that my new granddaughter, Hazel Louise, will benefit from the knowledge within these pages.

About the Author

Jan M. Schmuckler, former professor of organizational psychology and director of the Coaching Certificate Program at J. F. Kennedy University, developed the concept of role montage while writing her doctoral dissertation in 1978. For more than thirty years she has used the idea with her coaching and consulting clients in the Silicon Valley and beyond. Jan lives in Oakland, California, with her husband, children, and granddaughter.

Connect with Me

Website	www.janconsults.com or www.rolemontage.com
Email	jan@janconsults.com
LinkedIn	https://www.linkedin.com/in/jan-schmuckler-7ab2135
Facebook	https://www.facebook.com/janconsults
Goodreads	www.goodreads.com/book/show/29605040-role-montage

Notes

1. Lillian Cartwright was dean at the California School of Professional Psychology when I was completing my dissertation.
2. John P. Kotter, *Leading Change* (Harvard Business Review Press, 2012), 15,161.
3. A. Colman and L. Colman, *Love and Ecstasy* (New York: The Seabury Press, 1975), 72.
4. C. Musselwhite, "Self Awareness and the Effective Leader," *Inc.com* (Oct. 1, 2007): printed 6/11/13.
5. R. Heifetz and M. Linsky, "A Survival Guide for Leaders," *Harvard Business Review* (June 2002): 71.
6. Edie Seashore was a pioneer in the field of organizational development, a past president of National Training Laboratories (NTL) and an active consultant. She died in February 2013.
7. D. Goleman, "What Makes a Leader?" *Harvard Business Review* (November-December 1998): 95–96.
8. D. Goleman, "Leadership that Gets Results," *Harvard Business Review* (March-April 2000): 80.
9. H. Gardner, *Frames of Mind: The Theory of Multiple Intelligences* (New York: Basic Books, 1983).
10. P. Salovey and J. Mayer, "Emotional Intelligence," *Imagination, Cognition, and Personality* (1990), 185–211.
11. D. Goleman, *Emotional Intelligence: Why It Can Matter More Than IQ* (New York: Bantam Books, 1995).
12. K. Bennett, "Madame Chairman," *Working Woman* (May 2000): 30.
13. S. Sandberg, *Lean In: Women, Work, and the Will to Lead* (New York, Alfred A. Knopf, 2013), 150.
14. J. M. Schmuckler, "Role Montage: Discovering Leadership Influencers," *The 2012 Pfeiffer Annual Training* (2012): 93–100.
15. N. Ozaniec, *Basic Meditation* (London: DK, 1997), 8–9.
16. T. Nhat Hanh, *The Miracle of Mindfulness* (Boston: Beacon Press, 1996), 41–49.
17. S. Boorstein, *Don't Just Do Something: A Mindfulness Retreat* (HarperSanFrancisco, 1996), 8–9.
18. J. Kabat-Zinn, *Wherever You Go There You Are: Mindfulness Meditation in Everyday Life* (New York: Hyperion, 1994), 3, 93, 131.
19. See https://zmm.mro.org/teachings/meditation-instructions/.
20. See http://www.dalailama.com/messages/compassion.
21. R. Heifetz and M. Linsky, "A Survival Guide for Leaders" *Harvard Business Review* (June 2002): 73.
22. C. Seashore, E. Seashore, and G. Weinberg, *What Did You Say? The Art of Giving and Receiving Feedback* (Columbia, Maryland: Bingham House Books, 2011), 3.
23. C. Musselwhite, "Self Awareness and the Effective Leader," *Inc.com* (Oct. 1, 2007): printed 6/11/13, 2.
24. M. Ruderman and P. Ohlott, *Standing at the Crossroads: Next Steps for High-Achieving Women* (San Francisco. Jossey-Bass, 2002), 153.
25. MBTI personality inventory is used to make the theory of psychological types described by C. G. Jung understandable and useful in people's lives. The actual inventory was developed by Isabel Briggs Myers and her mother, Katharine Briggs, to make the insights of type theory accessible to individuals and groups.

26 David Kolb published LSI, his learning styles model, in 1984 from which he developed his learning style inventory. Much of Kolb's theory is concerned with the learner's internal cognitive processes.
27 Thomas-Kilmann Conflict Mode Instrument, TKI, is a conflict style inventory, which is a tool developed to measure an individual's response to conflict situations.
28 See http://fp.eng.ua.edu/100/FILES/MBTI-PSI.pdf.
29 See www.eclecticenergies.com/enneagram/test.php.

www.ingramcontent.com/pod-product-compliance
Lightning Source LLC
Chambersburg PA
CBHW080412300426
44113CB00015B/2491